THIS FEMININE WORLD

Books by Mrs Robert Henrey

THE LITTLE MADELEINE (*her girlhood*)

AN EXILE IN SOHO (*her adolescence*)

MADELEINE GROWN UP (*her love story and marriage*)

A FARM IN NORMANDY (*the birth of her child*)

MATILDA AND THE CHICKENS (*a winter on her farm*)

A JOURNEY TO VIENNA (*the making of a film*)

PALOMA (*the story of a friend*)

MADELEINE'S JOURNAL (*London during the Coronation Year*)

A MONTH IN PARIS (*she revisits the city of her birth*)

MILOU'S DAUGHTER (*a winter in the Midi*)

BLOOMSBURY FAIR

THIS FEMININE WORLD

In America *A Farm in Normandy* is published under the title *Madeleine Young Wife*

From a portrait by Eduardo Malta

THIS
FEMININE WORLD

by
MRS ROBERT HENREY

LONDON
J. M. DENT & SONS LTD

FOR
MARY AND
ALURED DENNE

I

THEY were both delightful—the man small, dark, bubbling over with intelligence; the woman pale, exotic, wearing with infinite grace the appearance of extreme docility. I knew at a glance that their friendship would provide something strangely new and exhilarating, and I went forward excitedly to greet them.

'M. and Mme Eduardo Malta!' said my hosts. 'We shall have to talk French because they are Portuguese and neither as yet speaks more than a word or two of English.'

Mme Malta was small, wore a close-fitting velvet dress, and looked up at me (I was slightly taller than she was) with dark brown eyes that gave a serious, almost sad expression to a white and strangely oval little face in which a long, straight, but delicately drawn nose was the most arresting feature. Though everything about her was youthful, her hair, to my surprise, was grey, if indeed one can describe as grey that changing colour that fluctuates between steel-grey and silvery violet; and this vigorous, thick hair, brushed well back, revealed small, well-shaped ears whose exposure, together with her thoughtful expression, gave her at times a boyish look.

'What is curious,' said her husband, 'is that although I am sixteen years older than Dulce my hair is still jet-black, so that I am tempted to believe that she has monopolized all the lighter tints to keep them away from me. Whatever the reason, I adore my wife's hair. I have painted it so many times that I know its every mood and reflection.'

Until now the work of this portrait-painter, considered by experts to be one of the most brilliant in Europe, one of those most likely to be remembered by posterity, had been entirely unknown to me. His portraits of King Alfonso of Spain, Primo de Rivera, President Vargas of Brazil, Count and Countess of Paris, King Umberto II of Italy, and Dr Salazar are masterpieces, and it came as a shock to me that I should only just be learning about them. This was his first visit to England. Hitherto he had not thought it essential to travel much beyond his own country, Spain, Italy, and Brazil. There was something defiant in his refusal to take his genius out of his natural environment, but the fact that I was ignorant of his work made me appear in a bad light. It was as if a Portuguese woman had never heard of Augustus John. He was here, he said, to paint a Dutch oil magnate, and later he would go to a country house near Gloucester to paint a certain lady in waiting. Then back to Lisbon because Dulce was already lonely without her cats. His laboured French was amusing and picturesque. He did not think he would ever speak coherent English, but Dulce, who, being a woman, was quick and clever, might learn to speak it for him. This dark man, with the youthful neck and dark, probing eyes in a jocular face, looked somehow as if he did not quite belong to the age in which we live. His person, like his painting, was evocative of more colourful times. On the table there was an album of reproductions of some of his paintings, and as my host showed them to me I knew that I was looking at the work of one of the great masters. We went to a Greek restaurant in Percy Street because Alured Denne, our host, a senior executive of one of the great oil companies, had lived many years in Athens, and both he and his wife Mary spoke Greek fluently and had a great affection and nostalgia for the country. During the meal I told M. Malta how much I should like to watch him at work, and he invited me to come the next morning to the furnished rooms they had taken in Ryder Street, St James's, where from ten o'clock onwards he would be putting the finishing touches to a new portrait of Dulce.

'Spectators do not disturb me in the least!' he exclaimed, with what struck me at the time as a touch of bravado, but which I later came to see as no more than a frank acceptance of his amazing gift. There was no timidity about him. During the whole of this first meal his every reference to his art was positive, even dogmatic. That alone interested him. Though his features were full of character, I was curious to see the transformation that would take place as soon as he found himself in front of a canvas armed with palette and brush.

'My career started at the age of three,' he said. 'One day in Covilhã, where I was born, I saw a man riding a bicycle, and this amused me so much that on my return home I made a drawing of it which I took to my father, saying:

'"Look what I saw in the street!"

'"Who drew this for you?" asked my father.

'"Nobody. I drew it myself."

'"If you want me to believe you," said my father, "take this pencil and let me see you draw it again."

'I borrowed his pencil and made a second drawing, which my father put in his pocket and later showed to my uncle, but as my uncle proved as sceptical as my father had been I was obliged to make a third drawing—and so on until I had convinced the whole family. I drew as other children play with their bricks. With the help of my sisters I franked envelopes with home-etched postage stamps which, to our delight, reached their destination.'

I could not at a dinner-party question the painter as I would have liked. Behind these amusing tales there must have been others of a grimmer nature. But what a situation

for the parents, who discovered in their child of three unsuspected signs of what amounted to genius!

'I was painting portraits at eleven!' he said.

Then, hearing our host talking of the ramifications of
trade and supertax, the painter asked me in a whisper:

'Do you have to pay income-tax too? In Portugal we
are allowed to spend everything we earn. I feel in England
like a man who has stepped off a space-ship on to another
planet!'

At ten the next morning I crossed Green Park on my way
to Ryder Street. Raindrops fell from the naked boughs of
the plane-trees, but the earth smelt good with the promise
of spring. A postman in front of Lancaster House was
washing down a pillar-box. Clean curtains were being
hung in the tall narrow windows of that part of St James's
Palace which had been occupied by the Duke of Windsor
when he was Prince of Wales. Assuredly spring was on
the way!

Mme Malta, wearing her black velvet dress with a velvet
hat trimmed with a pale pink peony, welcomed me at the
lodgings in Ryder Street and said:

'My husband is already at work. Come and see what
progress he has made.'

The room, whose walls were freshly painted in grey, was
small, and in the middle of it stood the portrait on a heavy
easel. The artist was painting her against a grey background which toned with the room.

'That is my own tint of grey,' he said. 'I had the walls
repainted. They were cream, but it would have made me
uncomfortable to live in a cream room, and our parents
were right to choose warmer colours against which to hang
their pictures. I began this portrait of my wife on Sunday,
having discovered that in London there is nothing else to

do but work on Sunday. I am lucky to have my favourite model always at my side. I never tire of painting her.'

I looked from the portrait to Dulce seated beside it—and back again. The resemblance was incredible. I wondered what they would have said about it in Paris, where painters are still preoccupied with the abstract. I thought for a moment 'It is like a reflection in a mirror!' but it was much more than that. The portrait, despite its severity, had the warmth of life breathed into it. Was it because the artist had painted her so often that he was able to achieve this miracle?

Dulce herself had not at first struck me as beautiful, but I began to ask myself if there were not something of the Mona Lisa in her smile. I could not decide whether it was gay or sad. I wanted desperately to know her better.

The artist, seated on the edge of his stool, was at this moment stabbing the canvas with tiny flecks of pink. He was adding life and colour to her lips. After every stab he swivelled round to face his wife, thrusting his head forward like a great black bird searching out its prey, turned his dark eyes upon her to discover some new detail which with another stab he could transfer to the canvas. He was drunk with the joy of artistic creation. Never had I seen a man so excitedly alive; by comparison his features at dinner the previous evening had been like a mask. From time to time he emitted in pungent, ungrammatical French some statement designed to challenge my intelligence and to discover if I were worth talking to. To what other painter's work did I liken his painting? Had I studied the portraits by Ingres at the Louvre? Chardin was a painter he much admired. Did the National Gallery still own that fine painting by him of the little boy in the yellow coat?

I began to notice that he was reproducing on his canvas the exact shade of Dulce's lipstick, and I told him how Wilfred de Glehn, R.A., a disciple of Sargent, claimed that to do this was incompatible with true art.

'Why?' asked Malta.

'No woman was ever born with lips this colour,' I explained, pointing to Dulce's portrait.

'What do *you* think about it?'

'I think he was wrong and you are right.'

'Though I paint in the tradition of the great masters,' said Malta, 'why should I not give Dulce the colour of the lipstick she momentarily favours? By the time I next paint her portrait, even if it is only in a fortnight's time, she will doubtless have changed her lipstick, but the new one will be just as charming. Let us not argue about trifles. The personality of the sitter is what counts. One must go beyond the features to the soul.'

'Is that really possible?'

'Of course, otherwise it would be better to employ a photographer.'

Though our conversation was sometimes interrupted when the artist searched impatiently for words, or when he poured out his ideas in Portuguese to Dulce, telling her imperiously to translate them for my benefit, which she always did with amazing patience—in spite of these difficulties, all three of us were stimulated by this first meeting at their lodgings in Ryder Street. The speed of his painting, his complete assurance, and the novelty in outlook of these cultivated people who had suddenly arrived with the naïveté of medieval travellers on the confusing English scene—all combined to delight me. I found it exciting to watch this man painting in the classical style. I tried to make him talk about the impressionists and the surrealists. He respected the leaders of these movements, who had very understandably revolted against the form of painting laid down by the old masters, but now the world, he suggested, might be a little tired of the so-called moderns. Perhaps the inevitable swing of the pendulum will bring us back to something approaching the classical or rococo styles. In this respect he himself might be for all he knew the most ultra-modern of contemporary painters. Somebody always has to be ahead of the others.

He discussed the French romantic writers. He had been told they were popular in England. The Germans also greatly admired them. Germans were incurably romantic. He had discovered this in Lisbon and even more so in Brazil, where German bankers and writers had come to him to be painted.

'In what way did you find them romantic?'

'There was a young German who came to me one day, saying that his wife was in hospital expecting a baby. He wanted to present her with a portrait of himself as a great surprise. The painting had to be a secret between us until after the baby was born. He dreamed of the moment when he would make the gift. He was not rich. Would I allow him to pay a little now, the rest later? I agreed, and the portrait was a great success. A few months passed and then the young wife called on me. Would I paint her portrait? This also must be a great secret. She wanted to give it to her husband as a surprise. As for my fee—well, she would go without pretty clothes for a while. Now, that is what I call romantic!

'The French have become cynical. French people no longer think it fashionable to have their portraits painted. Spaniards are different. Though cruel they are gay. The Portuguese——'

'The Portuguese,' put in Dulce, 'are not gay. I once took dancing lessons with a Russian who said to me: "I have been in many countries, in Germany, in Poland, in Austria, in Britain, in France, and everywhere the people were different from my own, but as soon as I arrived in Portugal I found a sister people with similar characteristics —nostalgia, a sense of tragedy, a lack of gaiety, and a great deal of naïveté!"'

2

'MY MOTHER was twenty the day I was born,' said Eduardo Malta. 'I have not yet painted a single portrait of her, though it was she who from the beginning believed in me. My father thought that no man could make a decent living out of painting. Worse still, I wrote poems, and this vexed him, though in his own way he also was a poet. He passionately loved flowers and spent so much time growing them that he began to neglect the factory he owned.

'My interest in poetry earned me my first commission. I painted the portrait of Teixeira de Pascoais, the Lusitanian poet, who unwisely called me the greatest painter in Portugal, so that I was fired with ambition and ran away to Lisbon.

'My mother now lives in Oporto and never wears anything but black, for in a single month she lost my father and my married sister, Olinda.'

The artist had turned his attention to the peony on Dulce's hat. I sat on the edge of a small sofa just behind him in a corner of the tiny room. Every time he turned his gaze from the canvas to his model seated on her low chair, my own eyes moved in the same direction. There was a bow window with a window-seat. Through a curtain of heavy rain one could see the houses on the other side of Ryder Street. I wondered if it were merely coincidence that had brought the painter to this corner of eighteenth-century London, so near to where Swift shared his lodgings with his Stella, and where Sir Richard Steele, George Crabbe, and Thomas Moore had lived in bachelor's apartments. A small but fairly powerful lamp fastened to the side of the window threw its beam on to the canvas. I continued to question the painter and his wife in an attempt to penetrate their thoughts. I had heard it said that there were fewer great painters to-day because of the levelling effect of compulsory education. Clearly this Portuguese master had from the age of three done little else but paint. What else mattered? How often are a child's natural gifts stifled by our mania for standardization? As a boy had he other hobbies?

'I do not remember having toys,' he answered. 'I wrote poems and stories for the fun of illustrating them. I was never tired of drawing and painting. After my first childhood visit to the theatre I designed scenery for imaginary plays. The circus enchanted me, and even to-day it remains my idea of an earthly paradise. In my boyhood the arrival of a circus was a tremendous event in villages and small towns. When I was four or five I used to spend hours looking out into the street pretending that one of the shop windows at the corner contained a miniature circus, and every night I dreamed about it so vividly that I knew exactly how it was set out. This dream became so much a reality for me that in the morning I would jump out of bed to see if my miniature circus had taken shape, and the disappointment at never finding it still makes me rather sad. Dulce hates circuses, and is miserable when I drag her to one. She is so fond of animals that she is vexed to see them performing at the crack of a trainer's whip. She is convinced that at some stage of their training they are made to suffer.'

'Our home in Lisbon is a delight because of our pets,' said Dulce. 'I am not even sure that my first grey hairs were not directly due to the death of a favourite Siamese cat. Our dog is rather old, but our little maid takes good care of it when we are away. Fortunately we have no servant problem in Portugal. When my maid first came to me there were moments when she looked sad, and when I asked her what was the matter she told me she was unhappy at the thought that her widowed mother now lived all alone. "Bring her along," I said. "We can always find something for her to do, but I will pay her rather less than I pay you. She will at least have a comfortable home and you will be together." So her mother came to live with us, and I do not regret it, because when Eduardo and I are away our home in Lisbon has a family living in it—and our pets are well looked after.'

This young woman under her black velvet hat, dutifully sitting for her portrait, was as gentle as her name implied, and I looked so often from her to her picture that I seemed to know her twice over. I asked her how she met her husband, but it was he, not she, who answered:

'It was her sister who first attracted me. We met at an evening reception and I immediately longed to paint her. She agreed to sit for me and brought Dulce along, but though Dulce was not nearly so pretty I found myself becoming much more interested in her than in my model. She was amazingly intelligent, with a touch of arrogance that pleased me, and then, since in Lisbon everybody knows everybody else, I remembered having been introduced to the parents and seeing Dulce as a plump little girl running up the steps of the Rue Haute.

'Every time I look at my wife I find something new to admire in her. When a woman is too beautiful a man is tempted to search for defects. Besides, what is beauty? Love alone creates it. Love is the wonder of wonders.

'My father loved his flowers. I once knew a man who grew orchids. He owned one of those rare species which produce a flower every seven years. Well, the seventh year arrived and the man, overcome by joy, brought me the flower as if it had been his first-born, so that I should paint it.

'Men are as vain as women, perhaps more so. Dr Salazar, one of the most remarkable men of his generation, having given me permission to paint him, was anxious to be shown wearing a favourite collar of his which he had bought in Paris. He had his home turned upside-down for this treasure, but alas, the maid had lost it!

'Another distinguished sitter looked at the portrait I did of him and said: "Are you certain, M. Malta, that you have not made me appear younger than I really am?" In fact, I had not, but I think that like a pretty woman he was fishing for compliments, so I said to him: "If you insist I will do my best to make you look just ten days older!" So taking my brush I added a speck to his brow.'

'Does a portrait ever fail to please?'

'Of course! Sometimes it fails to please me; at other times it does not please the sitter. People who know nothing about painting occasionally ask for a detail which is artistically wrong. Others want me to give them more hair, or add frills or jewels. Then I cease to like the picture. A Norwegian woman, whose sixteen-year-old daughter I painted in jodhpurs, took a dislike to the canvas, which she put in a corner and did not pay for. I asked her to send it back to me, which she did, but when a few weeks later it was exhibited in a gallery and sold to a museum she was vexed to have parted with it, and wanted me to make her a copy, but it was my turn to be vexed and I refused.'

'The portrait is finished!' cried the artist to Dulce. 'You may come and see it.'

With an air of quiet satisfaction he signed the canvas, after which, at the top right-hand corner, he added a

B

scorpion, eighth sign of the zodiac, a mark only to be found on pictures that particularly pleased him.

Finally he removed the canvas from the easel and slipped it into a frame to enjoy what Ingres once called the artist's supreme recompense—the sight of his picture framed.

3

EVEN before Dulce's picture had been varnished the artist invited me to take her place beside the easel, wishing, I think, to prove to me that though I had only just come into their lives he could put what he called all my hidden self on canvas as easily as in the case of Dulce, whose portrait he had painted over forty times.

Dulce therefore took my place on the sofa, a writing-pad on her knees and a box of chocolates at her side, for she guessed that her husband would work long past the lunch-hour, and that it would not be easy to find a restaurant in London willing to serve hungry people with an omelet after three. Her own portrait hung framed on the wall. I admired in particular the magnificent study he had made of her back, bare because of the old-fashioned *décolleté* of her black velvet dress, with its long tight sleeves. The little dimples in her back gave this splendid picture an adorably naïve quality.

My features were now the ones to be probed by the artist's dark, laughing eyes, and though he hardly ever paused in his work, except to jump up and consider it from a distance, a much greater intimacy had grown up between the three of us, and I took advantage of this to question the painter more minutely about his boyhood. What did he really think about the compulsory education we now gave our children? Was it a good thing?

'For many, yes—an excellent thing; but certainly not for a painter!' he exclaimed. 'Students go to art school these

days at eighteen, but by the age of eighteen I had already
studied for eight years at the Oporto Fine Arts School.   It
is not nearly enough for a child to show a marked gift for
drawing, as I did at the early age of three.   A promising
beginning, perhaps, but a clever drawing by a child of that
age too often has an element of luck about it.   Good workmanship requires technique, and that, as I need hardly point
out, is a matter of constant application.   At eighteen, with
much hard work behind me, I could afford to indulge my
fancy by flirting with all the different schools of painting,
trying to copy each in turn.   I have read that the great
English poet, Alexander Pope, before discovering a style of
his own, the style which distinguishes his genius, copied all
the most celebrated poets of his day.   In painting, this
process can go on till a man is thirty, after which he should
be ready to adopt a line of his own.   Time is all-important
for a painter.   He must start working very young.'

'Tell me more about your boyhood.'

'My tales of school life are different from those of most
other men.   For instance, having carried off all the prizes
for drawing I had to start painting nudes, but I was only
eleven and the rest of the class were grown men, many of
them with beards.   They laughed at me a good deal.   I
was such a serious little boy.   Some of them, anxious to
pull my leg, succeeded in making me believe that after I had
painted a nude model I would have to kiss her legs and
thighs.   I was so terrified that for two nights I never slept,
and yet I knew that I must attend these classes which were
vital to my work.

'The models were not chosen for their shapeliness or
beauty.   Tired flesh hung loosely about them and their
bosoms had long since lost their youthful tone.   When at
last I found sufficient courage to enter the room I blushed
with shame.   For a very young boy this first sight of the
naked female body, not in its bloom but in its decadence,

is a horrifying experience. However, what in the first moment of panic had struck me as ugly did not seem so for long. I quickly discovered new wonders, new effects of light and shadow, and my eleventh year finished in a sort of rapture.

'There was a girl of about sixteen whom I was soon to meet at morning lectures at the university. She worked much harder than I ever thought it possible for a girl to work. Her long blonde hair fell in waves about her shoulders. She wore what are known to-day as ballerina shoes, and when she passed in front of me I noticed that her heels touched the ground before her toes, in a way that put me in mind of a Greek goddess. Learning that she attended geometry lectures in the afternoon, I also put my name down for them, and I spent my time following her from lecture-room to lecture-room. Not once did I declare my love, but I was not the only one to be smitten by her beauty. A young student came out of a lecture one day, gave one long look at her, and then shot himself dead.

'This girl, called Lucinda, who inspired so much love, never married. We all loved her, but the others were no braver than I was when it came to declaring it. We were too young, too pure, too chivalrous. There is, however, a tender, poetic side to calf love which doubtless proved excellent for my painting.'

Dulce smiled indulgently. She was writing a long letter to her mother in Lisbon.

'I have to make it long,' she explained, 'because my mother will take it round to my house and read it to the servants, who simply adore letters, though none of them can read or write. Their great joy also is to send letters to their friends and relations. I am obliged on these occasions to play the part of public scribe. They group themselves round me and I begin: "What do you want to say to your Aunt Maria?" After a moment's silence I receive the answer: "We cannot put our thoughts in order, but you, our mistress, who know everything, just write what you think we should like to say!" So I write the letter, and when I read it out to them tears roll down their cheeks and they exclaim: "How beautiful! How beautiful!"'

Dulce looked at her husband and said:

'I must telephone to Mother this evening to ask about the cats.'

M. Malta, without pausing in his work, explained for my benefit:

'My wife once had a Siamese cat which we both adored. We called it Menina, and it was so intelligent that we felt certain that it must have been a bewitched princess as in a fairy-tale. Menina's affection for my wife was terrifyingly exclusive, and this beautiful animal prevented anybody from approaching her. Certainly its reactions were often human. When occasionally I would go and lean over the balcony that juts out into our street, the Siamese would run off to fetch Dulce as if it feared I was going to commit suicide, and nothing would calm it till I was safely back in the drawing-room.'

'It expected me to amuse it,' put in Dulce. 'We often played hide and seek together, but if I sewed or knitted the little wretch would jump up on the arm of my chair and try to take the work away from me. If I still went on it would spring on my shoulder and slap me.

'When I undressed at night Menina would hide under the bed, but as soon as I was ready to slip into it, one foot on the floor and the other raised, Menina would make a dash for the one on the ground and try to imprison it. Then the wise and lovable creature would jump into the bed, cover us with kisses, and nestle down between us.

'At heart, I think, it loved Eduardo as much as it loved me, but it rather hid its love for him as if it feared that I might be jealous. When the cat and I were alone I used to talk to it as I would have talked to a human being, and one day when I was reading in an arm-chair and the cat was on the floor it suddenly sneezed, and unconsciously I called out "Santinha!"—"Little saint!"—which is equivalent to saying "God bless you!" in English. My dog Joaninha was devoted to it, though in principle it loathes cats, and when Menina fell ill the dog was in a terrible state. One evening, after Menina had hidden itself in a corner all day, it came up to bed as usual and kissed me more fondly than ever. I was delighted. I thought my darling Menina must be better, but a few hours later it died.

'I was too broken-hearted to have another cat, but I have adopted a whole colony of wild cats that live on the roofs of our Lisbon street which is picturesque and narrow. I first saw them from my balcony as they prowled between the chimney-pots. Nobody knows how the first ones got up there, but they have multiplied, and as far as I can tell none of them ever ventures down. Perhaps there is no possible descent. They live on the roof tops like marooned sailors on a desert island, and until I took them under my protection they were half starved. At six o'clock every evening they come to a certain spot opposite my balcony and I hurl their carefully prepared supper across the chasm that divides us. My maid or I send fish or meat flying from roof to roof. We need to be careful, for imagine what would happen if sardines or roast beef were to fall on the heads of unsuspecting passers-by! Occasionally one of my adopted tribe, after a brief absence, reappears at the appointed place with half a dozen kittens in a line. Others that cease coming at meal-time never return. Have they slipped and been killed, or have they discovered some way to climb down into the street?'

'Cats and dogs are like humans,' said her husband, suddenly joining in the conversation. 'There is always the odd one more intelligent than the rest. When, during my trip to Brazil, I was painting Princess Maria Thereza de Bragança, sister of the Countess of Paris, I sometimes had to wait in her home till she came in from some engagement. She had a little dog to which she was devoted, and when the dog and I were in the same room I would say to it "Go and look at your mistress!" and it would go to my easel and contemplate the canvas. A dog would be unlikely to recognize somebody from a photograph, but an oil-painting with its human proportions and lifelike colour is a different matter.'

I asked Dulce how the letter to her mother was getting on. She was telling her, she said, about their morning walk down Bond Street. She and Eduardo had eaten an early breakfast and were out exploring the streets by nine. They had discovered a shoemaker in Clifford Street in whose window Eduardo, to his great excitement, had seen a pair of shoes that exactly resembled those his father always wore. Not since his father's death had he seen shoes of that particular shade.

'Alas!' said the shoemaker. 'I would find it very difficult indeed to make you a pair of shoes of that colour, because the ones you admire have been in my window for over thirty years. Exposure to air and sun has given them that golden tint. They are a poem!'

'I am sorry,' said the painter. 'I shall have to choose a more modest pair.'

'Alas!' said the shoemaker again. 'We have practically no more craftsmen left. I could not make you a pair of shoes under six weeks.'

'I am Portuguese,' said the painter, 'and in six weeks' time I hope to be back in Lisbon.'

'You are Portuguese?' cried the shoemaker. 'Then let me shake you by the hand, for I owe a great debt of gratitude to your country. When I reached Portugal in 1940, miserable and penniless, having escaped from German-occupied France, your people, learning that I was English, said to me: "Our country is yours!" They lodged me, fed me, took me for drives through the vineyards, and loaded me with grapes. How kind they were! No, I shall never be able to repay the Portuguese!'

'Are you, like most Latins, sentimental about your parents?' I asked M. Malta. 'Do you think of your father with great emotion and love?'

'I do now,' he answered. 'I judge him less harshly, but I am ashamed to think how many years it took me to see him in the right perspective.

'I must confess that I inherited my mother's jealous nature. One does not become jealous; one is born that way. My father was not in the least jealous, but my mother was madly so.

'My mother was jealous of every woman who looked at my father; my sister and I were jealous of the flowers that absorbed so much of my father's attention. We used to blame those unfortunate flowers for everything that went wrong. When money was short we used to say: "Well of course, we know why!"

'For many years I never looked at a flower, and when I sent people flowers it was because I was obliged by the rules of courtesy to do so, but even now I seldom give flowers to Dulce, and you will not find any in my home in Lisbon. Childhood prejudices are not easily overcome, and deep down inside me there remains, I suppose, a touch of bitterness; but I no longer bear a grudge against flowers as such. Indeed, I am not sure that I am not indebted to them for a good deal of my talent as a painter.

'If my father had not brought about our ruin by his love of flowers, I would certainly not have worked so hard from earliest boyhood. To carry off first prizes in painting became an obsession with me. The child that I was

became a bundle of ambition, bravado, and pride. My
natural talent was sharpened by the adversity which over-
took my father.   Pride, I feel sure, is a necessary ingredient
in the character of a young man who wants to get on.   One
often hears a man blamed because he has a high opinion of
himself, but would he have climbed above the crowd
without it?

'A man's capacity for hard work, if it is to become second
nature with him, is best developed by the stimulus of want
or hurt vanity.   Nevertheless, family reverses and family
quarrels provide a sad background for a child.   My father,
when I was far too young to understand such things, sent
for me one day and said:

'"Eduardo, if you love your mother, don't leave her for
a single moment to-day."

'He added, placing his hand affectionately on my
shoulder:

'"Go now, my boy, and do as I tell you."

'I hung about my mother's skirts all day.   Her bitterness,
her eyes red with weeping, her deep and frequent sighs,
broke my heart, as I witnessed in silence every meta-
morphosis of her consuming jealousy, that most cruel and
sterile of all afflictions.   That was the day when I should
have painted her.   My mother now lives a tranquil life
with my unmarried sister.   Her dead now belong to her
alone, so that no pangs of jealousy any longer assail her.
I myself have learned to think of my father in a new light.   I
am beginning to collect and to love certain objects which
I associate with him.   This will help you to understand
with what emotion I saw that pair of shoes, so like the ones
he used to wear, in the shoemaker's window in Clifford
Street.'

Dulce, as dainty as a doll in a cashmere twin-set the

colour of Parma violets, was kneeling on the cretonne-covered bow-window seat looking down into Ryder Street. Suddenly her husband, in an almost harsh voice, called out to her. He needed some colour on his palette. Dulce, calm but agile, jumped down, and taking the correct tube inquired on what part of the palette she was to squeeze out the colour.

'I see that you have trained her!' I cried, laughing.

'There's no longer much for an apprentice to do,' said M. Malta. 'In the old days when colours had to be pounded in a mortar it was a different story. I buy these in Belgium from a firm which for generations has made the same sort of colours as were used by the great masters, and they do the work that was originally done by apprentices. The firm closed down during the war, and I would have run out of these exquisite colours if chance had not brought the great artist Kisling to my home. Like the shoemaker of Clifford Street he was fleeing from the Germans, and as soon as I learned that he was in Lisbon I offered him hospitality. His only luggage was a case of colours from the makers in Belgium, but when, after many weeks' delay, he was finally able to fly by Clipper to New York, the case of colours had to stay behind, and so he made me a present of it. Thus I was able to go on painting right through the war.

'A painter is accustomed to his own colours. He has his whims. This russet-coloured coat, for instance, which I bought in Biarritz seventeen years ago, has almost become a necessity to me when I am painting. Dulce has several times tried to make me exchange it for another, but I slink off to my cupboard to fetch this one. I call it my talisman.'

4

I HAD suggested to the Maltas that we should take a morning off to visit Hampton Court. This met with immediate approval. A Portuguese poet had apparently described this historic place in a celebrated poem which Eduardo knew by heart. Dulce was in favour of a very early start. In Lisbon she was always out of the house by nine because of the intense midday heat.

My husband offered to drive us there and we set off in high spirits. Dulce had insisted that we should drive slowly. Her stories of Lisbon taxi-drivers made her qualms understandable. They and their colleagues in Rio de Janeiro, she said, drove so recklessly that from time to time, feeling faint, she would ask them to stop. 'Invariably when I pay them off,' she added, 'they look at my waist, supposing that only an expectant mother could be so nervous.'

M. Malta, muffled up in a fur coat, was in the back talking to Antonio Lopez Ribeiro, the Portuguese film director, whom we had picked up outside the gates of Burlington House. Dulce in front, between my husband and myself, warmed our hearts with tales of her sundrenched land, of the excellent fish she served with home-grown rice, and of her countrywomen who so seldom wear anything but black, even when they go to a friend's house to dance. 'My friends all thought I must be mad,' she said, 'when once at a dinner-party in Lisbon I wore a bright red evening dress which I had bought during a trip abroad with my husband.'

The car ran smoothly over Kew Bridge, past Kew

Gardens whose pagoda was half shrouded in winter mist. The Thames at Richmond, the deer in Bushy Park, light snow on the grass, frozen puddles, that first enchanting glimpse of the warm red brick Tudor chimneys of Hampton Court Palace—these were some of the many wonders I wanted Dulce to see before she returned to her homeland.

Though the sun broke out to welcome us, it was bitterly cold as we emerged from the last courtyard into the gardens. The thick ice on the pond had been broken in the centre for the benefit of the ducks, who waddled and slithered across the unbroken part to reach this enticing pool of cold, clear water. This sight so enchanted M. Malta that he would, I verily believe, have come all the way from Portugal just to witness it. We lunched at a riverside inn in front of which, in spite of the cold, an old man was playing a small harmonium. The painter hurried across to him, conversing with him for a few moments in broken English. Then with the utmost respect the painter slipped a note into the musician's hand.

After lunch we went back to the palace to visit the apartments. Dulce had told me when we first met what an exhilarating experience it was for her to go to the Prado or the Louvre in the company of her husband. I now enjoyed a similar privilege. How simple and yet penetrating are the explanations of a man who has learned every detail of his art! For a moment he remained pensive before a Titian. 'No jewels, no frills, no background,' he murmured, as if trying to justify his own views on this question. 'All the character confined to the face.'

We went also to see the paintings of Andrea Mantegna, the fifteenth-century Italian artist, whose panels of the Triumph of Julius Caesar, housed near the Great Vine, did much to inspire the pre-Raphaelite movement in England a century ago. English critics have for so long found it fashionable to praise only the French impressionists, and to pour scorn on Burne-Jones, Dante Gabriel Rossetti, John Millais, and G. F. Watts, that I found it strange to hear this Portuguese painter expounding a more balanced view. I recalled that when he and Dulce had looked in for a moment at our apartment near Piccadilly, he had examined with interest a Watts portrait of Lady Lindsay, a member of my husband's family, playing her Stradivarius. Did not Watts also have an old smock which he could not part with, and which he affectionately called Squalid?

As we came out of the palace the sun bathed the Tudor herb garden in a rosy glow, though icicles hung from the fountain above the lily pond. An aeroplane droned overhead.

'That must be the Lisbon mail plane!' said Dulce with sweet naïveté.

Punctually at ten the next morning I climbed the stairs of the house in Ryder Street. The apartment door was open and two carpenters were busy replacing the lock. Hearing my voice, Dulce, in a grey cashmere two-piece with a white schoolgirl collar, came out on the landing and said in her quiet voice:

'We had a burglar yesterday while we were out. The cupboard and the chest of drawers in the bedroom were ransacked and all our clothes thrown on the floor, but evidently the burglar did not find what he was looking for because nothing is missing. Perhaps he wanted money.'

'The paintings?' I cried. 'Your portrait and mine! Are they safe?'

I was thinking of the theft of the 'Mona Lisa.'

'They are safe!' said M. Malta, beckoning me in. 'The stupid fellow gave himself all this trouble for nothing, but would you believe it, all our friends are telephoning us from Lisbon. The Portuguese newspapers printed the news.'

We left the carpenters to their work. This was my final sitting and the painter was anxious to finish my portrait before lunch. Dulce went to kneel on the bow-window seat so that she could look at the pigeons and the London sparrows who came for the bread she distributed to them every morning.

After a while she said reflectively:

'I wonder if I should write to Mother again and ask her to keep an eye on the refrigerator. The maids always forget to keep its door closed.'

Eduardo smiled enigmatically. Dulce rose, offered me a chocolate, and explained:

'My maid, who is so clever at some things, has the brain of a sparrow in other respects. She is amazingly clever at cooking Portuguese rice, for instance, but mechanical things like refrigerators baffle her. She is the prettiest little thing, exquisite and fragile, but so small that I think that men are afraid to ask her to marry them. They probably fear that she would not be strong enough to do the rough work in a home and rear a family. Her life with us is very different from what it would be if she were to marry, and though she still cannot read or write she has developed a very sure sense of what is beautiful. That tends to keep her in a world apart.'

'Naturally,' said her husband. 'The same applies to too much beauty in a woman, or too much intelligence. They tend to isolate her. Take Lucinda, for instance, that lovely and clever girl I was telling you about. She never married. Did I not tell you also that I preferred Dulce to her more beautiful sister?'

I was about to object that at least Dulce had inspired forty of his finest portraits, when Dulce herself broke in:

'Eduardo is right. I had two sisters, one of them more intelligent than I, the other prettier, but my father, whom I adored, used to say: "Dulce, you are the nicest!" The girls at school used to tease me because they said I was too serious, and one day when I told this to my father as we were crossing the great square in Lisbon, he pointed to the statue of the Marquis of Plombal and said to me: "You look like him, my little Dulce!" I was delighted. Though the marquis must have had many crimes on his conscience, he was a national hero and our most famous square was called after him.

From time to time I was allowed to get up and inspect my portrait. A hand with the fingers held slightly apart had just made its appearance, but the other was not yet born, and Dulce, sensing a slight hesitation in her husband's mind, declared that in her opinion the hand that was about to be painted should be gloved.

'As in the famous Titian at the Louvre!' cried Eduardo. 'What a good idea! Go and fetch a glove, Dulce!'

She went to fetch one of her own white gloves and in due course my second hand took shape thus clad. The painter had become very gay. The unexpected turn the portrait had taken gave him the same sort of elation as a glass of wine. We were glad, Dulce and I, because he was so obviously happy. The master was pleased with the picture.

During lunch at the inn near Hampton Court, Antonio Ribeiro had talked to us enthusiastically about a trip he had just made across the North American continent. 'America is the place to go!' he had cried, but though Eduardo Malta had painted a number of distinguished Americans in Europe he remained silent when asked if he would like to go to New York. This question now came back into his mind, and turning to me he asked suddenly:

'Would you like to work in New York?'

I answered that, quite apart from my inclinations, there were such problems as income-tax and dollar exchange, and the fact that even if I did go to America I might not be capable of earning my living there. The best solution, I thought, was to offer my services as personal maid or cook to a millionaire. An American woman with whom I had crossed to Paris recently had startled me by the fabulous wage she said she was obliged to pay her Swiss maid, and this woman had added: 'I have also given her a motor-car, and of course she has all my shoes and dresses after I have worn them a couple of times.'

The painter's eyes shone with delight.

'Why go by yourself?' he cried. 'Let us hire ourselves out as a team—you, Dulce, and I! The Gugenheims are millionaires. They might employ us. I painted Mrs Gugenheim's portrait some time ago. We shall need your husband also because he is the only one of us who knows how to drive a car, and that, according to your informant, appears to be indispensable. I could write and say that Dulce is an excellent cook and that you would be willing to act as a personal maid.'

'What will be your role, Eduardo?' asked Dulce.

'Serve at table and dust the old masters,' he answered. 'Then we could write a book about our experiences illustrated with portraits of our employers. The main thing is to prove to ourselves that we all have a second string.'

There was silence for a few moments except for the rasping sound of the brush against the canvas as the painter filled in the background. A pungent smell of paint filled the small room. Dulce, who had curled herself up on the sofa to write to her mother, looked up and said:

'I must buy a handkerchief for Mother. I promised to send her something every day in my letter. A handker-chief is such a sweet messenger. I should like to think that as soon as she opens the envelope it will fly out like a kiss!'

'There!' cried the painter. 'The portrait is finished. Come, both of you, and look at it!'

C

5

AS the fabulous Mme Suzy Volterra, after winning the 1955 Derby with her horse Phil Drake, curtsied to the Queen, who exclaimed to her: 'I have never seen such a sensational finishing burst!' the band at Epsom, to the delight of tens of thousands of racegoers, struck up: 'If you knew Suzy . . .!'

Suzy, the blonde, beautiful widow of Léon Volterra, whose photograph she carries about with her wherever she goes, shares with the tall, elegant Begum Aga Khan the distinction of being the best dressed and most romantic of French women owners. If anybody were to ask me why I am so supremely happy to be a woman I might give the Begum Aga Khan and Mme Suzy Volterra as examples of the heights to which feminine intelligence can lead one.

To the Queen Mme Volterra said: 'Your Majesty, I am so very happy, not just because my horse has won the Derby, but also because he won it in my husband's colours. It is the best memorial I could give him.'

Léon Volterra is to-day a legend. Born in Algeria, he went to Paris as a lad of fourteen, earning his living by opening cab doors outside a theatre. Then with some money borrowed from an uncle he started a theatre-ticket agency, and eventually controlled the world-famous Folies-Bergères, the Casino de Paris, the Marigny Theatre, the Lido, the first night-club to have a swimming-pool, and Luna Park, the great Paris fun fair which rivals Coney Island. Léon Volterra's career reads like a tale from the Arabian Nights. A man offered him a very undistinguished

racehorse for £300. 'What is the animal called?' asked
Volterra. 'Roi Belge,' said the man. 'I will buy it,'
answered Volterra. A few weeks later Roi Belge won at
40 to 1 at Auteuil.

Suzy Volterra's success story is no less incredible than
that of Léon, but it has something else—the addition of
femity that makes it even more tremendous. Suzy's
story is not merely one of an astonishing rise to fame;
there is tragedy, poignancy, immense all-conquering love
for the man who was—and still is—all to her. The love
she bears her husband, who died in 1949, is the motive
power in her glittering existence.

He first saw her dancing on the grass at a floodlit midnight Longchamp race-meeting that he himself had
arranged. We shall allow her to tell this story herself in a
moment. It was not till May 1947 that they were married.
Léon Volterra had reached the height of his career. Mis-
tinguett, Maurice Chevalier, Raimu, Dorvill had at some
time or other come under his powerful influence. He had
achieved all his ambitions except one, and that was to win
the Derby. To win the Derby had for long been a dream.
In 1938 he had owned Bois Roussel—but he sold it a
fortnight before it accomplished its historic win.

In 1948, the year after he married Suzy, he had a part
interest in two Derby runners—My Love and Royal Drake.
The Aga Khan had the other interest in My Love, and it
must have been the larger interest because the horse
carried the Aga Khan's colours. My Love came in first
and Royal Drake was second. For Léon Volterra that was
indeed an amazing achievement but it was not, strictly
speaking, a Volterra victory. The winner had not carried
his colours. The day was the Aga Khan's.

Léon Volterra was still confident. Then came the
poignant drama that caused him, on the point of death, to
believe he had won the 1949 Derby.

Armour Drake was the horse.   He believed in it and he
was the sole owner.   Unfortunately he was very ill from heart
trouble and the doctors would not let him travel.   He asked
Suzy to represent him at Epsom.   Suzy travelled to England
by steamer, but the doctors cabled her that Léon had taken a
turn for the worse and she had to rush back to Paris in a specially chartered plane.   Her husband was dying and Armour
Drake had been beaten in a photo finish.   Once more, by a
hair's breadth, the Derby had eluded Léon Volterra.

'Knowing how much the Derby meant to him,' said
Suzy, 'I told him a white lie in the hope that he would get
better.   I told him he had won the Derby.'

He smiled contentedly.   Suzy's white lie brought him a
ray of happiness on his death-bed.   She lied out of her all-
embracing love, a very tiny lie because, if the photo finish
had not been invented, Armour Drake would undoubtedly
have shared in a dead heat for first place.

At all events Léon died in the belief that his horse had
won the Derby.   Suzy was determined that one day her
husband's colours would be carried to victory.   Therein
lies the key to the words she uttered to the Queen in 1955:
'Your Majesty, I am so very happy, not just because my
horse has won the Derby, but also because he won it in my
husband's colours.   It is the best memorial I could give
him.'

When Suzy went back to her London hotel she placed a
picture of Phil Drake beside her husband's photograph,
and entwined both with his racing colours.

Just before this magnificent victory, Suzy had been told
by friends in London that the Aga Khan, who was staying
in Piccadilly and had a horse of his own in the Derby,
thought Phil Drake would win.   When this was repeated
to Suzy she exclaimed:

'This indeed is a happy sign. The Aga Khan brings luck.'

The Aga Khan did not go to the Derby. He remained at the Ritz and sent the beautiful Begum.

'Why of course, my little Madeleine,' the Begum said to me in her apartment at the Ritz the day following the race. 'I am quite delighted that Suzy won the Derby.'

She added:

'Suzy earned her success. She worked so very hard for it. So many people think that owning racehorses is just a big game. Well, it's nothing of the kind. It's a deadly serious business—and one in which you must on no account lose your head.'

The Begum was in the middle of packing. She and the Aga Khan were leaving by air for Zürich. Freda, the Begum's faithful Swiss maid, kept on bustling in and out, trying to remember which of the bags were to go to Switzerland and which were to be sent direct to Paris to await the arrival of the Princess.

At this time I had no idea that our rather scant references to the Derby would eventually lead me to Suzy Volterra—and to the Derby winner, Phil Drake himself, not in Epsom but in Chantilly. For the moment the Princess, Miss Dorothy Ginger, her English lady in waiting, and Freda talked about Cannes whence they had all come. The Aga Khan's magnificent villa at Le Cannet, above Cannes, is called Yakymour—a combination of Yaky (the Begum's name) and *amour* (love). The Cannes Film Festival had just ended, and the Begum was saying that what she liked best about it was the opportunity it gave of going to a film in a different language every day. She and the Aga Khan had entertained many of the visiting film-stars at Yakymour, including Lollobrigida of whom the Begum said: 'I found her charming.' Now they were flying to Zürich, and from Zürich they would go to Paris.

'The Aga Khan adores travelling,' said the Begum (he was in the adjoining room with the door open!). 'He can't stay still in one place for more than a few days. He is so tremendously young in his interests. All kinds of different subjects fascinate him, and he simply must keep himself up to date.'

I am never tired of admiring the Begum. All the papers carried photographs of her and Suzy Volterra at Epsom. On this particular afternoon, as she sat in the middle of a number of half-packed suit-cases, the Begum was wearing a navy-blue pin-striped tailor-made, a dark red carnation in her lapel. Her lovely features were tanned by Riviera sunshine. From time to time she darted out to talk to the Aga Khan in the adjoining room. Then she would return and continue the conversation.

Because of their imminent departure I did not stay long. She noticed on my bracelet a gold coin she had recently sent me from Mecca where she went as a pilgrim, for she had embraced the Aga Khan's faith. She said: 'I looked in all the bazaars for presents to send to my special friends, but I found nothing. The pilgrims who go to Mecca are not rich. Then I went to the bank to cash a cheque. They paid me in gold. So I said to myself: "Here are my presents from Mecca!"'

We spoke about our respective mothers, both in France. The Begum had recently visited my farm in Normandy to see my mother; her own mother has a house near Yakymour. As we talked, a sparrow came in from Green Park and perched just inside the room. It had a green leaf in its beak as if it were returning to Noah's Ark.

A week later the Aga Khan and the Begum were in Paris,

having stayed only a few days in Zürich. I also was in Paris and I said to her:

'I am terribly intrigued by Suzy Volterra. Do you know her well?'

'Does that mean you would like to meet her?' asked the Begum.

'If she is in Paris,' I answered.

'She is at Chantilly,' said the Begum. 'I will ring her up and ask if you can go and see her.'

That is how I set forth to visit Suzy Volterra.

6

PARIS was bathed in almost tropical sunshine. Mme Suzy Volterra telephoned me from Chantilly. 'I am here to rest,' she said, 'but I am also very sad. This is the anniversary of my husband's death. However, if you are alone, please come out and visit me.'

I walked as far as Christian Dior's in the Avenue Montaigne. To most people Christian Dior means the A-line —but to me his shop is a bus stop. The conductor cried out 'Christian Dior!' as his London counterpart might cry out 'Green Park!' or 'Haymarket!' So I boarded a bus at Christian Dior's and rode to the Gare du Nord.

When my train arrived two elegant women were waiting on the platform at Chantilly. One of them was very tall, the other, I recognized immediately, was Suzy Volterra.

'How sweet of you to come and meet me yourself!' I cried out.

She was wearing a blue print dress with a red design. It had no sleeves. Her shoes were white. Her companion had what was the very latest fashion in Paris, a sleeveless tweed dress of a cut that looked simplicity itself until one tried to copy it.

We drove off in a large blue car to Mme Volterra's villa, and soon were seated in the cool of her drawing-room, furnished in the English style with gay chintz curtains.

There was a very serious expression on her lovely features. I remembered reading how for a long time after her husband's death she became known on the racecourses of Longchamp and Auteuil as the Sad Lady. People claimed they never saw her smile.

'Yes,' she began, reminding me of what she had said on the telephone, 'this is 5th June, the day my husband died. I am always quite alone when this anniversary comes round. The drama comes back to me so vividly. He was so hopeful that he would win this 1949 Derby with Amour Drake, and indeed when the crowds were waiting for the result of the photo finish nobody knew that he had not won. There was never any question of my husband being present at Epsom. He had been ill for nearly a year. When I was summoned back to him I was so anxious to give him a chance of getting better that I said:

'"Bob, you have won the Derby!"

'I always called him Bob when we were together. Oh, if only my white lie had been able to restore his health, or at least give him a few more weeks or months. Still, it is wonderful to think that I won the Derby with a descendant of Amour Drake which, alas, came in only second in that 1949 Derby.'

Mme Volterra paused, and then continued in a strangely soft voice:

'After my husband's death I went to see the Aga Khan. He knew that I was broken-hearted and alone, and he was afraid for me. I said to him: "I *must* keep my husband's racing colours!" I was so emphatic that the Begum exclaimed:

'"But naturally, Mme Volterra, naturally! And I am quite certain that one day you will win the Derby in your husband's colours."

'Then the Begum turned to the Prince, her husband, and said:

'"After all, *you* won the Derby!"

'So you see, Mme Henrey, I have a tremendous gratitude to the Begum because she encouraged me at that fateful moment. That is why, in another sphere, I have such admiration for your lovely young queen. Her responsibility is enormous, and she carries out her duties with such courage.'

Suddenly Mme Volterra's features were convulsed. Her lovely eyes filled with tears that streamed down her cheeks.

She said:

'Do you know what I have been doing? I have just laid on my husband's grave a big bunch of white and red flowers—his racing colours; and chose the same coloured flowers for his son's grave. He had a son who was killed at the age of twenty-one in a motoring accident. He used to say to me: "Suzy, my son would be your age now—and I am quite certain he would be in love with you!"'

When she had dried her tears I sought an answer to the riddle of her own beginnings. So many stories have been told, that she was a singer, a dancer . . .

'I was born in Paris,' she said, 'but because I had a young cousin who was a dancer at the Opéra, it was decided that I should be one too.

'I became what in France we call a *rat de l'opéra*—a young dancer; and while I was dancing I attended the school which all the dancing girls go to. There I passed my School Certificate.

'Was I sorry to leave off dancing? Not entirely. Of course, I was passionately fond of it, and I was extremely quick to learn the technique. Think of it! I danced with Yvette Chauviré, France's *première* ballerina, for whom you in England have so much admiration. She came over with the Paris Opera Company to Covent Garden recently.'

The villa at Chantilly was very modest. I might have been in any small country house near Ascot or Sunningdale.

It belonged to her trainer, François Mathet, a young cavalry officer who graduated second at St Cyr and first at the cavalry school of Saumur, and who taught her a great deal of what she knows about racing. Mathet, having a family of his own, has taken a larger house. This one was sufficient for her.

What struck me was the way the former ballerina of the Paris Opera House had applied herself to the business of horse racing. I recalled the words of the Begum Aga Khan in London when she said to me: 'It's a deadly serious business.' The Begum should know something about it, for she had this in common with Mme Volterra, that she had to begin at the outset of her marriage to make herself mistress for the first time of all the intricacies of horse breeding and racing. Once at Deauville, with fascinated interest, I watched the Begum walking round a yearling sale. She is quite as clever in this respect as her husband or Aly Khan.

Suddenly Mme Volterra exclaimed:

'I adore the Riviera, and my husband and I built a magnificent home for ourselves in the sun. Then, when the house was finished, he died. So I could not bring myself to live in a house which he and I had planned to turn into a love-nest—a house like the Begum's Yakymour. I do not therefore go there any more.

'The same thing happened in Paris. He and I lived in the Avenue d'Iéna. I would not go there again. To-day I live in the Avenue Marceau.

'There is only one place where I am happy in my memories—that is at the Savoy in London. We used to hold hands as together we looked at the swiftly running Thames, and we would formulate our wishes for the future, dream a wonderful dream about winning the Derby!

'In London I am almost happier than anywhere else, and

I shall tell you a secret. I love to buy shoes there. There is something quite special about London shoes. Besides, everybody is so kind to me in London. They all seem to expect me when I arrive, and the station-master at Victoria presented me with a magnificent bouquet on my return. I received scores of letters from people who had backed Phil Drake—and one letter from a real Phil Drake, a man whose name that was. He won a little money on the race by backing the horse that had the same name as himself—and he wrote to me: "If your horse has a filly will you please call her Sheila because that is my daughter's name."'

'Were you very poor when you became a girl dancer?'

'My father was killed in the First World War when I was a baby so I was brought up by my mother. We were not well off but I was an only girl and she spoiled me. From the moment I began dancing fortune smiled on me. I have been applauded, loved, given absolutely everything that a woman could desire. I do not think there are many women alive who have had such a magical life.

'My husband was to me a father, a husband, the very light of my existence. He adored extremely feminine women. I might even say that the women he liked best were those he considered in need of protection. He was perfectly aware, of course, that dancers and actresses work hard, but he used to say that even the most famous and successful dancer or actress is not quite sure of herself, that she invariably needs a man to love and help her. "Elles sont quand même faibles!" he would say.

'I rode quite often when I was first married, side-saddle with a top-hat or a bowler hat, but Léon simply could not do without me. I mean that he wanted me continually beside him—so I was obliged to give up my riding. As you know he had come to Paris as a poor boy, and though his career was like a fairy-tale he suffered hard blows. But he used to say to me:

' 'When things go really badly, never admit it. Pretend you are doing fine. Ill luck never lasts. The bad moments in life are always over more quickly than the good ones.''

7

THOUGH Suzy Volterra's drawing-room at her villa at Chantilly was small the sun played brightly on the red chintz curtains. A photograph of Léon Volterra, her husband, who in her thoughts still presides over the destinies of the house, was very prominent, and I had the curious impression that he was looking at us and listening with interest to our feminine voices.

'See, Mme Henrey,' said Mme Volterra suddenly. 'I will show you something I only show to my very close friends.'

She took the photograph of her husband out of its frame and gave it to me so that I could read what Léon had written in a big masculine hand across the bottom: 'A mon grand amour—à ma petite Suzy.'

To my Great Love—To my Little Suzy

A moment later Mme Volterra was called to the telephone. In her absence, intrigued by a magnificent silk scarf lightly fastened to the handle of her hand-bag, I untied it and discovered that it bore the design of all the Derby winners since 1780. In the last square, the one at the bottom left-hand corner, I read:

Phil Drake
owned by Mme Volterra
by Admiral Drake
out of Philippa
ridden by F. Palmer
trained by F. Mathet

My eyes roved to the scintillating names elsewhere on the scarf—the Maharajah of Rajpipla, Lord Derby, Lord Rosebery—and my friend, the Aga Khan. What dreams are conjured up by this amazing company of men and women who obtained, some once, others such as the Aga Khan more than once, their dearest wish.

While the scarf was still in my hands, Suzy came back into the room and said:

'A friend in Paris sent it me this morning. It was flown from London. I treasure it more than if it were a diamond necklace worth thousands of pounds. Yes, literally. I do not, in my position, need to wear magnificent jewels. My pearls are sufficient. They never leave me. I have come to consider them as part of my personality.'

They were indeed magnificent, her pearls—two rows whose milky, rosy splendour seemed to radiate a living force against her bronzed skin.

'Furs are what I love!' she exclaimed suddenly. 'Furs and big hats! Look! This is the sort of hat I adore wearing. It is made in the form of a halo—what we call in French *une auréole*; and I repeat that I love *auréoles* in spite of the fact that I was beaten by the Queen's horse of that name. Well, what greater honour could I have than to be beaten by a horse belonging to the Queen?'

Mme Volterra asked suddenly:

'Would you mind coming up to my bedroom? I am worried about Gris-gris, my Persian cat, who would not eat his lunch!'

She took me by the arm and we hurried to her room.

'Ah!' she cried. 'Here is my darling Gris-gris. See how green are his eyes! They are the same colour as my own.'

We were standing by the balcony, and in the full light of this magnificent afternoon I noticed for the first time that her eyes were in truth green! Not only were they green

but they had that slight upward slant that beauty experts
call 'cat-shaped eyes,' which just then were so popular in
young and pretty women. The heat was so intense that
Gris-gris was stretched out at full length. He had a collar
from which hung dozens of charms like the charms that we
women so often hang from gold bracelets round our wrists
—and I noticed that one of these charms was a tiny coronation coach! Lazily Gris-gris got up, followed us deeper
into the room, and lightly jumped up on to Mme Volterra's
bed; and I was reminded of Simba, the blue Persian I
chose for the Begum in London, which had become such a
favourite with the Aga Khan ('We are both Persians!' he
had said, laughing) that it was generally to be found on his
bed, or the Begum's, in the same way as Gris-gris was now
on Mme Volterra's. These Persians, incidentally, both
have pedigrees as long and as distinguished as that of any
Derby winner!

'Now,' said Mme Volterra, 'I will show you the favourite
of my favourite hats. I wore it at the Derby. It is a halo
of sapphire-blue straw, extremely light, becoming, and
easy to wear.'

She quickly put it on her head and turned to look at
herself in the mirror.

'Here is another which I wore at the Prix de Diane—a
halo like the first, but its colouring is the blue of a corner
of sky on a beautiful summer's day. How do you find it?'

'You have what the French call *une tête à chapeaux*!' I
exclaimed. 'A head on which every hat looks beautiful.'

'I am faithful in my loves,' said Mme Volterra. 'Mme
Lemonnier always make my hats just as Balmain makes my
dresses. I am not the sort of woman to go to this great
couturier or to that one just because he or she is in the news.
The most important thing for an elegant woman is that she
should not feel worried about what she is wearing. If I,
for instance, were preoccupied about the dress or the hat I

was wearing at Epsom or Ascot, I could not give all my attention to my horses.

'When Queen Elizabeth spoke to me the other day after I had won the Derby I was very nervous—first because I had just won the greatest race in the world, and secondly because any woman would be nervous when spoken to by so young and beautiful a queen. There was a third reason that made me nervous. My first words to her were: "Forgive me for not speaking better English, Your Majesty, but I speak with *all* my heart!" Then I suddenly thought of my husband Léon, and how I wished he could have been standing there in my place talking to the Queen!

'My husband, as everybody knows, came to Paris as a poor lad and made a vast fortune and a great name—a legendary name. He was at home in all sorts of different worlds. His success was due to the fact that he remained perfectly simple, perfectly understanding of other people's troubles, and sufficiently intelligent not to allow anything to turn his head. He considered that any job well done represented achievement. Now, come and see the room where I keep my dresses.'

We went into the linen-room, the room where her dresses hung. On a table was a jockey's cap with her famous red and white colours—the white was of superb poplin.

'My own personal maid looks after them,' she said lovingly. 'These colours are, to my mind, the most beautiful in the world. The red is a geranium red. That is why when I went to the cemetery to place flowers on Léon's grave, I chose red and white geraniums so that he should know that it was for him I won the Derby.'

The jockey's blouse lay beside the cap. My feminine mind was already making a plan. I will use this design when I knit my next cardigan. I will wear it with a white pleated skirt. My face lit up with anticipation as I

D

expounded my plan to Mme Volterra, who answered, beaming:

'Oh, I am so happy that you also love the combination of the two geranium colours—they are so simple, so chic! I must, of course, admit that since they have been crowned with such sensational success I love them even more. Life often needs great courage. After Léon's death, on that occasion when I went to see the Aga Khan and the Begum, I was faced with a great decision. To be or not to be! That line kept coming into my head. Was I to carry on? Or was I not? What has happened now proves that the decision I came to was the right one. But it did not seem (except to the Begum Aga Khan) so very right then. Everybody tells me now that I was right, and that they would have done the same thing in my place, but that is being wise after the event. If I had sat down in my corner and cried, what would have become of me? I did the exact contrary. To many people I appeared a far too merry widow. My apparent gaiety, my love of clothes and racing, often hid a sad and weary heart. Let others profit by the success which has come to me because I refused to give up.'

8

I WAS standing with Mme Suzy Volterra on a wide balcony at her villa at Chantilly. Gris-gris, her Persian cat, seated on the balcony rail between us, gazed thoughtfully with his green eyes across his mistress's domain towards the distant powdery road leading to the famous racecourse. Beneath us was a fine rectangular courtyard with two magnificent lawns, and all round were horse-boxes. Men in white overalls were painting a piece of the projecting roof, and the fresh dark green paint shimmered in the hot sun.

'I am having that piece of roof painted,' said Mme Volterra, 'because just now there are no horses underneath. The smell of paint would certainly upset them.

'I am grieved to say that thoroughbred horses do not, in my experience, like the perfumes that flatter our sex. They do not appreciate our expensive scents or the smell of powder and lipstick. When I was newly married, and knew practically nothing about racehorses, I was not aware of this important fact. My then trainer did not dare tell me. He was wrong. When a thing is true you should be implacable—especially when it concerns animals. There is no middle way.

'I do not want to let you go before I have shown you Phil Drake, but first you must come and taste some of the cream from my farm, the farm where my horses are born and where I send them when their racing days are over so that they can enjoy the peace of family life.

'As you also own a farm in the rich pasture lands of

Normandy, I do not need to tell you that with so many horses and cows we have no need for chemical manures. I flatter myself that our cream can stand comparison with any in France. Now come with me. I have asked my cook to serve us with a very light meal before we go off to visit Phil Drake.'

We took our collation in a very airy room under the picture of a horse. The cold beef was excellent, the cream a real poem. Then I asked:

'What horse is pictured on the wall?'

'That,' answered Mme Volterra, 'is Roi Belge—Belgian King.'

I answered:

'Oh, of course, I have heard of him—the horse your husband bought from a man who did not think much of him?'

'Yes. Roi Belge, until my husband bought him, had not brought much luck to his owners. My husband bought him mostly on account of his name. Roi Belge reminded him of his theatre in Brussels. However, the horse won him some useful races, and I never saw my husband pass the picture without looking up at it with a loving expression in his eyes. Those of us who own race-horses are surprised how quickly and truly we become attached to them, almost more so than one would like.'

The little dining-room was furnished entirely in the English style. There were red and white flowers everywhere.

'You must forgive me,' said Mme Volterra, 'if I continually bring my husband into the conversation. I never take any decision, even the most trivial, without asking myself if it would please him. That, of course, surprises people very much, but I am what you might call a marked woman—marked indelibly by the memory of my husband. He was much older than I—and supremely intelligent.

Intelligence is a much rarer gift than is generally supposed.
The Princess Aga Khan is one of the world's most fortunate
women because she has a supremely intelligent husband.
Léon Volterra and the Aga Khan are men who set a mark
on their women for life. The brains of such men are
irreplaceable.

'When I was leading Phil Drake into the paddock after
his victory I was surrounded by famous people, but I only
had one impression—a feeling of intense loneliness.

'We first met in a fairy-like setting—a night of pure
enchantment that would need the pen of Grimm to conjure
it up. One day I may be tempted to write a Thousand and
One Nights of my own. All this proves that fairy stories
happen in all ages. Never believe that the tale of the
shepherd girl who marries the prince cannot happen
to-day. The proof is that it happened to me.

'My husband had launched a midnight race-meeting at
the beautiful Longchamp racecourse. The most perfect
summer's night contributed to this amazing sight. There
was music and there were side-shows—and all the most
elegant women in Europe in their loveliest dresses, with
diamonds and furs. Léon Volterra had dreamed this
fabulous dream, and made it come true. The ballet of the
Paris Opera House was invited to give a performance under
the floodlit trees.

'There was tremendous competition amongst the dancers
to be chosen for this spectacle. Just imagine the thrill it
is for a dancer to perform in the open air under a canopy of
stars!

'I was one of the girls to be chosen. In our ethereal
white dresses we danced the ballet of the Blue Danube.
Dancing on a lawn is not at all easy. Our toes were apt to
sink slightly into the turf, but no woman could ask for

a more magnificent moment than when thousands on thousands of people turn towards her and break into tumultuous applause. How could I possibly guess that in this immense crowd that was cheering our ballet there was just one man who was applauding for me alone?

'For Léon Volterra it was love at first sight, like a thunderbolt. For me it was the beginning of an entirely new existence—a life that I could not even imagine. The heavens opened for me on that brilliant summer night at Longchamp. I was swept to the winning-post.

'I did not entirely give up dancing at the Opéra but I began to go to race-meetings—more and more of them. Now, enough of my love story. Come and see my Phil Drake.'

We entered the courtyard through a magnificent door, the sort of door one might expect to find leading into a convent. In the sixth box on the right was the victor who was waiting for us, having immediately recognized his mistress's voice and step. I found him handsome. Mme Volterra stroked him with the tips of her fingers but he seemed so tall to me that I dared not follow suit. On his name plate I read:

PHIL DRAKE
sired by Admiral Drake
from Philippa de Hainaut,

and I cried out: 'How curious! Was it not Philippa de Hainaut who implored her royal husband to save the lives of the six bourgeois of Calais?'

I loved Phil Drake all the more for reminding me of this piece of history learned in girlhood. Eagerly I followed Mme Volterra from box to box and into the harness-room. For the first time since my arrival there was a smile on her face.   Her features were as clear and bright as the sky of this perfect summer's day.

'I am expecting twenty-five births!' she exclaimed.   'I so adore them when they are babies.   Just think of the fun of having a nursery of twenty-five foals!'

9

IN Mme Suzy Volterra's bright blue Cadillac we drove
up to the tree-shaded square of Chantilly. The heat
was so great that we might have been at Cannes.
There were cafés with big orange-coloured parasols,
and Mme Volterra told me that as soon as she had been
to see her trainer she would go for a swim.

I was obliged to go back to Paris, so we parted at the
station with its flowers and white railings. She called out:
'I also shall be in Paris to-morrow. Ring me on my
private line. I want you to see my apartment.'

I watched the blue Cadillac speed off in the direction of
her trainer's house. Just as her husband's racing colours
were red and white, so Mme Volterra had a colour which I
shall always associate with her—the blue of her Cadillac.
What one might call the Suzy Volterra blue.

In the very heart of Paris, at the Étoile, there was a
magnificent modern apartment house all faced with marble.
On the first floor lived Mme Volterra.

She was not there when I arrived, but had given instructions to her personal maid to entertain me by showing
me her hats and dresses. I was to be let into the secrets
of her wardrobe, which Parisians claim is amongst the
most fabulous in France. This news gave me more
pleasure than if I had been invited to see the treasures of
Aladdin's Cave.

Her maid came forward to meet me with Gris-gris, the

Persian cat, tail up, at her heels, and she greeted me with the words:

'I am to take madame into madame's bedroom.'

The rooms of the apartment opened out into one another, and so off we went in a strange procession—the maid, Grisgris, and I—as if we were visiting the Palace of Versailles.

Mme Volterra's bedroom was adorable, with a bed in Suzy Volterra blue. The walls were hung with yellow satin which must have seen at least a century of existence. The wardrobe, which was large, was covered in the same satin, so that if it had not been for the mirror one might easily have confused it with the walls.

The maid opened the wardrobe with a smile in anticipation of the cry she knew I would utter.

Is this then what one requires to be an elegant woman in the most elegant capital in the world?

My eyes blinked. Here were the basic requirements of the woman of fashion—stockings carefully put away in neat little boxes as one sees them in the shops, gloves, hand-bags of rare beauty, and lingerie.

The night-dresses were so magnificent that at first glance I mistook them for dresses. Were there any in nylon? I saw none, but then when one has a maid so expert at washing and ironing real silk and hand-made lace one does not have to think in terms of what dries quickly and needs no ironing.

'There is *one* nylon night-dress which madame bought in America,' said the maid in answer to my query, 'but madame does not often wear it.'

On a couch sat a large doll, the sort of doll one would love to give one's daughter if one were a millionaire. The maid took it up, as she would a baby, and passing her hand under the doll's skirts straightened her petticoats.

Then suddenly the doll began to speak, telling us that sometimes she was good but more often naughty, that she was far too greedy, and often disobedient. Then she sang very softly.

'How does she do it?' I whispered.

'One buys small electric batteries to put inside her,' said the maid.

The maid and I listened solemnly to the doll as if we were two little girls in a story-book by Mme de Ségur—and between us sat Gris-gris in thoughtful contemplation of the eternal wiles of women.

The carpets were magnificent and Mme Volterra had them made to tone with the satin on the walls.

Her maid told me in a confiding voice that madame showed a preference for modern furniture in her Paris apartment. This struck her as a pity, because she, madame's maid, would have liked to be surrounded by antique furniture.

'I often tell madame that antique furniture is already so old that it does not seem to get any older. One can rely on what had given pleasure to succeeding generations.

'Now I must show you madame's boudoir, because it is entirely furnished with what she had in her dressing-room when she was a dancer at the Paris Opera House. You will see that I am right about old furniture being pretty, because this is all Directoire.'

The boudoir—a corner of theatreland brought into an elegant woman's apartment—was indeed enchanting. What delightful things one can do when one is both famous and rich! The sofa had so large a leopard's skin thrown over it, the teeth and claws were so fierce, that I involuntarily stepped back.

'You have not shown me Mme Volterra's dresses.'

'We are coming to them,' answered her maid. 'Madame's dresses are in her robing-room.'

In this room there were only cupboards. The maid threw several open to reveal a spectacular collection of dresses.

Those for the evening, mostly of embroidered satin, stood out as if they were already being worn. Some were embroidered in semi-precious stones. The white ones dazzled the eyes but there were delicate pale blues—the Suzy Volterra blue.

One also that surprised and enchanted was in the form of a sheath entirely composed of black and gold sequins mounted on black net, designed to make its wearer resemble a panther!

Balmain created all these dresses. I could have cried out in admiration at the genius he had shown with the tops of them, making them look like pieces of sculpture by Rodin. Merely to breathe on them, one felt, would be sufficient to see them spring into life.

Gris-gris jumped down from the ironing-board to quench his thirst at a dripping tap over a washing-machine, and then arched his back against my stockings, but he was all wet.

'Of course you knew the great Léon Volterra?' I asked the maid.

'Indeed,' she answered. 'He was always so gay even when he was very ill. He used to tell us stories about his boyhood in the streets of Paris. What a talker he was! Prince Aly Khan used to come and spend hours with him, just listening, and do you know what Prince Aly would do?

'He would sit at the foot of M. Volterra's bed, or sometimes even on the floor, and hold his hand. Yes, they would stay like that, hand in hand, for a long time while M. Volterra told Prince Aly stories.'

'M. Volterra was devoted to madame?' I queried.

'Yes,' she answered. 'You would never see one without the other, and he used to call madame "My little child."'

We talked about the Begum Aga Khan.

'She is the most beautiful of women,' said the little maid. 'And, madame, believe me, I have a great experience of beautiful women. Before being with madame I was with Mme Letellier and we used to go to England to visit Lady Louis Mountbatten.'

We walked out on the terrace, passing through a small room in which there was a television set. Among the flowers and shrubs on the terrace was a sculptured head of Admiral Drake, the famous racehorse from which Phil Drake was descended.

The blue Cadillac drove up at this juncture and Mme Volterra, in a navy blue striped costume, hurried forward to greet me.

LOOKING at the magnificent dresses in Mme
Volterra's wardrobe gave me a desire to go to
Pierre Balmain, who designed every one of them,
and see his summer collection. I rang up Mme
Nelly Normant, Mme Volterra's *vendeuse*, who
exclaimed: 'Why of course, Mme Henrey. Come at three
o'clock.'

But at two o'clock, while I was lunching in a small
Italian restaurant near the Madeleine, the intense heat of
the last few days broke into a torrential storm, and as I was
alone and without a car I began nervously to wonder what
to do and how to get to Balmain's without getting my dress
soaked.

A Florentine at an adjoining table then engaged me in
conversation, telling me that he had come to Paris to sell
Chianti wine, and that in a few moments the owner of this
restaurant, who was also a Florentine, was coming to talk
business with him.

'The man who owns this restaurant,' said the dealer in
Chianti, 'arrived in Paris not so long ago with twelve lire
in his pocket—and the address of a cousin who might
possibly help him; but when he traced his cousin's address
he found that the cousin had gone, so as he was tired, and
it was evening, he curled up on the doorstep of the empty
house and slept till morning. With only twelve lire in his
possession he had no fear of being robbed. I do not need
to tell you, madame, that he got a job next day and worked
so hard that he started a restaurant, then another, then

another. This is his third. There is another man from our home town who has done rather well for himself. He is a good friend of ours. We have known him since he was a little boy. If you have been in England lately you may have heard about him, a painter called Annigoni. I am told that the English are very enthusiastic about a portrait he has painted of the Queen!'

The owner of the restaurant, wearing the chef's traditional dress of striped trousers, white linen coat, and toque, emerged from the kitchen and came over to us.

'I was telling madame about our compatriot, Annigoni,' said the dealer in Chianti.

The restaurant owner nodded appreciatively, picked up some cherries from a wicker basket on the table, and tasted them thoughtfully.

'The cherries in Florence are juicier,' he said.

Three Indians drove up in a taxi, whereupon I implored Annigoni's compatriots to help me engage it, and with many farewells in Italian I drove off to Balmain's.

The collection had already started. The magnificent *salon* was bathed in the light of cut-glass chandeliers, and through open french windows one saw the rain pouring down from a black sky on to the Rue François Ier. Mme Nelly, who was very busy, placed me at the end of a row of chairs, and I found myself seated next to a little boy in a blazer who was absorbed in a comic. A sumptuous evening dress, richly embroidered from corsage to hem, swept past us like a great sea wave. Then the model who wore it stepped down from the raised corridor and disappeared into the models' dressing-room. As the door opened to permit her passage one caught a glimpse of girls in girdles and brassières, and others wearing voluminous petticoats.

A pretty blonde, with her hair done up in a bun and wearing the sort of summer dress that I should like to wear

at Deauville, was the next to come along the raised corridor.
As she passed us she looked down and smiled at the little
boy beside me.

When she had disappeared into the models' room I asked
the boy:

'Do you know the lady?'

'Why of course I know her!' he answered. 'She is
Mummy!'

He looked at me critically, obviously wondering if he
should confide in me further, then added:

'To-day is a half-holiday at school, so as it was raining
and I could not go out and play I had lunch with the
concierge, and Mummy brought me along with her.'

Here came a dress so heavily embroidered that I could
well imagine it being worn at the Louvre in Renaissance
days. The model who was wearing it smiled down at both
of us, and I asked the little boy:

'Do you like that dress?'

'Yes,' he answered. 'I like it.'

'Then you are interested in dresses?'

'I like dresses,' he answered, 'but I hate girls!'

As if to show me that my feminine conversation bored
him, he busied himself feverishly with his comic, and so
absorbed did he become that I even had to nudge him each
time his mother came along.

The collection ended. The little boy folded his comic
and stuffed it in his blazer pocket, for he was dressed like
a little English boy. A moment later Mme Nelly came
across to talk to me!

'You missed Mme Volterra!' she exclaimed. 'She was
here before lunch to try on a dress. I have a difficult time
making her keep still while she is trying on. She is restless
and does not particularly enjoy fittings, but her critical
sense is acute. She knows immediately, for instance, what
is wrong with a dress, and how it should be altered.

'We were the first to whom she telephoned from England after Phil Drake won the Derby. We love her because though she buys the most sumptuous of Pierre Balmain's creations, she remains extremely simple and nearly always comes to our annual holiday on St Catherine's Day. Last year all the seamstresses swore they would make her dance in the workroom. And she did! She danced a Neapolitan dance.

'I have never seen her tired. She seldom goes to bed before four in the morning, and twice a week she rises at five to visit her horses. On these occasions she will merely have time to change from some lovely evening dress into warm tweeds. Just now we are making her that magnificent dress the little boy's mother was wearing when you first came into the *salon*. The dress is called Rose of Paris, and now here are the measurements of France's most elegant woman:

Bust measurement	$33\frac{3}{4}$ in.
Waist	$22\frac{3}{4}$ in.
Hips	35 in.
Height	5 ft $4\frac{3}{4}$ in.

'These measurements are virtually those of a model.

'Now about slimming.

'She NEVER slims. She claims that she is far too energetic ever to be in danger of putting on weight. She eats everything she wants to.'

I bade farewell to Mme Nelly, who was born in New York but who was so French in appearance and spoke the language so perfectly that when I first met her I had not the slightest suspicion that she did not come, as I do, from Montmartre.

She took me to the door of the *boutique* and added:

'Really! Was it not wonderful about Phil Drake!'

PARIS, on this cold, dry Saturday afternoon, was deserted. Everybody seemed to have gone off for the week-end. I crossed the Place Vendôme, mounted the white steps of the Hôtel Ritz, and asked the porter to announce my presence to the Princess Aga Khan. He telephoned, and I heard the Begum answering:

'Be so kind as to ask Mme Henrey to come up.'

There was no need to inquire the number of the suite. One needed merely to know the number of the floor, because as soon as one stepped out of the lift one was quite certain to discover a picturesque group of the Aga Khan's faithful talking in low, reverent tones outside his door. They moved like shadows between pieces of luggage parked in the corridor, trunks that would comfortably house a family of large St Bernards. The luggage was marked in black letters: H.H. AGA KHAN. I had visions of staterooms in Atlantic liners, romantic journeys, colourful Eastern ports, poignant farewells at the quayside as the sirens wailed.

The Indian servants smiled in the friendliest way to me as with their dark hands they motioned me to the apartment, and I found myself being welcomed by the beaming, homely Freda who ushered me into the drawing-room where, seated on a ruby-coloured velvet arm-chair, was Simba, the Persian cat, who had lifted her beautiful head to see what manner of woman Freda was bringing in. Beside her a grey parrot remained so motionless in its cage that one almost doubted whether it was real.

Simba, having recognized me, signified by purring that I could stroke her. She seemed to be saying: 'I have not seen you since we played in the garden at Yakymour.' The grey parrot was also at Cannes. His immobility made him look precious and wise.

The Princess as she came in brought light and sunshine with her; her beauty laid a finger on everything. She was tall, which added to her presence, and the nobility of her bearing befitted the title of princess. Yet how sweet and gay was her smile, how easy to read in those eyes her immense kindness. As for her dress, I cried out in admiration.

Her dress was the colour of the deep blue cornflower. There are times when cornflowers picked in the fields run through all the gamut of shades. To visualize the colour of her dress you must think of the deepest cornflower blue, the blue of the flower at its most vigorous. The high neckline revealed three rows of pearls which nestled against her skin and were warmed to a rosy glow by it. One was tempted to believe that this was where they were born. Those who claim that there is no difference between real pearls and artificial ones have never seen pearls of this beauty. They blushed and shimmered, and gave added whiteness to the neck, which in return provided them with the living warmth without which they could not exist.

'The Prince and I are waiting to hear the official date for the postponed Ascot!' she exclaimed. 'I am hopeful that Military Court, which won the Lincoln, may acquit himself well in the Gold Cup. Should I send him? Should I not?'

Freda arrived with some umbrella covers. One was white, two were light brown, and the Begum was anxious for the brown ones to match the brown in her racing colours, but Freda said:

'What do you think, Princess? The two browns are not quite the same?'

'This one is the better,' the Begum declared, making her choice. 'No two whites are ever exactly of the same whiteness, so how can one expect two browns to be of the same shade? But I do hope nothing further happens to postpone Ascot. How can one imagine an English summer without Ascot? But come, let us have tea.'

The Aga Khan's big dog arrived. How frightened we were of him, the Begum and I, some years ago when one summer afternoon in London, on a sudden impulse, we set off to buy Simba.

The Aga Khan's big dog was our fear.

'He will kill the kitten!' the Begum exclaimed.

The following month they all went to Deauville. The Aga Khan, who hitherto had only liked large animals, horses and elephants, adopted the baby Persian, who slept on his bed, and the big dog roved the corridors of the Golf Hotel at Deauville sniffing under the doors for Simba. Then suddenly they came face to face. Simba did not spit and put out her claws. The dog, too, was on its best behaviour. Soon they became inseparable.

'There,' said the Begum to the big dog. 'Go and kiss little sister.'

The dog went obediently to Simba seated on the ruby-coloured velvet arm-chair, thrust his nose into her deep silky blue fur, and then jumped up on a couch beside her and put his head between his paws. Simba, as unperturbed as a Sultana accustomed to receiving homage, gently closed her golden eyes.

'As you are a good dog,' said the Begum, 'here is a piece of sugar! All the same,' she added, turning to me, 'he is difficult with most cats. I am ashamed of him when we are in the country. As for the parrot, do not be misled by his immobility. He has, on occasion, the most sardonic laugh. The other day, for instance, I received a letter from a bird club. I am well aware that there are clubs without number, but a bird club was something quite new to me, and when I commented on this aloud to the Prince, saying, "Does it not strike you as a little odd—a bird club?" before the Prince could answer the parrot broke out in a sarcastic laugh. Either he was surprised that I did not know about this club, or he was hurt that I should think it odd. The truth is that I am afraid of him. I feel certain he hates women!'

We talked about Egypt.

She and the Aga Khan showed an increasing affection for this land where they could be even more certain of hot weather than in the south of France. At Assuan, five hundred miles south of Cairo, the Aga Khan had chosen his tomb of rose-red granite.

'The Aga Khan wants to sleep in the hot sand overlooking the waters of the Nile,' said the Begum, 'and when I die I want to lie beside him. We do not want to be parted. But as we are not always thinking about death we have bought a villa at Assuan. It is delightful, though very simple.

'Our villa rests upon great blocks of granite as if it had been deposited there by some giant eagle which had flown over the desert with it in its talons. To reach it we must ascend a long stone stairway. I cannot tell you how beautiful it is. There is just enough electric current for the light—but for everything else, such as refrigeration, we shall use either gas or oil.'

I was strangely moved by the thought of this villa perched by an eagle on the rocks above the rose-red granite tomb which the Aga Khan and this beautiful princess who was talking to me had chosen for their last resting-place, near the catacombs where the Pharaohs buried their dead so many long centuries ago. I thought of the swarthy, picturesque figures waiting so patiently in the hotel corridor. They represented a tiny handful of the

millions of Ismaili Muslims throughout the world who
recognized the Aga Khan as their spiritual leader—a few
grains of sand in his immense kingdom. Hushed were the
voices outside the Prince's door. I had a sudden feeling
that time was standing still. My princess was as beautiful
as once Nefertiti was. Her profile was adorable and her
blue dress gave suppleness to her movements.

'I bought two embroidered handkerchiefs in Switzerland
the other day,' the Begum continued. 'Let us go half and
half. One for you and one for me—unless, of course, you
also are superstitious?'

'Yes and no,' I answered cautiously. 'In France, as you
know, there is a saying that handkerchiefs are for drying
tears. I am nervous for those I love.'

'You are right,' she answered. 'And I am afraid for my
parents whom I adore. I see them growing older and it
breaks my heart. Let us not have anything to do with
these handkerchiefs. My father is coming to Paris to
consult a doctor. He is eighty. Look! Here is a picture
of him. Is he not a fine looking man!'

She unfolded a leather photograph case which she carried
about with her everywhere, and I looked in turn at her
father, her mother, the Aga Khan when he was quite young,
another of the Aga Khan on their wedding day, and herself
at the age of two!

Every evening, from wherever she happened to be, she
telephoned to her mother and father, who lived at Cannes
in a house not far from Yakymour. My own mother,
since the first time the Begum walked down the orchard to
visit her in my Norman half-timbered farmhouse, had been
quite a different woman. She would not have been more
surprised if a princess had come to her from Mars. The
Begum's beauty, her natural elegance, charmed my mother,
who watched her sitting by the stone fire-place drinking
a glass of milk straight from the cow. The concern we

showed for our respective families was a bond between us. Our homes were six hundred miles apart. My farmhouse faced the English Channel. Yakymour was built on the flank of a mountain overlooking the Mediterranean. At Easter when the Begum wore a white dress and sat under her orange-trees in blossom, I walked in a tweed skirt and jumper through orchards bedecked with pear blossom like bridal veils.

The garden at Yakymour was not large, but in February it was full of oranges, lemons, and grapefruit. Prince Philip, who went there to visit the Aga Khan and the Begum during a recent stay in the south of France, fell in love with the place. Prince Aly Khan and Rita Hayworth found themselves besieged by the press there at the time of their wedding. 'One had the impression,' said the Begum, 'that there was a journalist hidden behind every mimosa bush.' This state of affairs so exasperated Rita Hayworth that one day she had herself rolled up in a thick Turkey carpet and spirited away in a furniture removal van right in front of the eyes of the world's newspaper reporters.

'Simply everything interests the Aga Khan,' said the Begum.

One of his great pleasures was to notice how when he entered a theatre or a restaurant in Monte Carlo, in Deauville, or in Paris, everybody looked admiringly in the direction of the beautiful tall woman by his side. He adored the presence and conversation of women. He listened with amused interest to the smallest details of the Begum's shopping expeditions or of her dress fittings. That is why she herself had become so superb a conversationalist. She knew that to interest him she must herself be interested in everything. Always learning, exploring new subjects, absorbing the points of view of fresh friends, going more deeply into the truths of her husband's faith, she had by now become one of the best informed women of her generation. She had, however, what I admired most in my own sex—a true sense of balance between feminity and intelligence. The fact that she went on a pilgrimage to Mecca did not prevent her from going into raptures over a ribbon or a new hat. That was, of course, an echo of what the Aga Khan pointed out in his famous interview on television, when he was asked how he reconciled a love of racing with his spiritual position. Appreciating the good things of life can be the mark of a religious man, he said. The parties he gave at Yakymour were in themselves proof of how he liked to keep abreast of what was going on—but he was careful to see that they invariably became triumphs for his wife. What was more wonderful for a woman than to have a husband who was always scheming to enhance her beauty and her wit? When Cannes celebrated a recent film festival the Aga Khan invited all the stars to Yakymour, where they found star-shaped fountains on the lawns in the jasmine-perfumed garden. When the grand ballet of the Marquis de Cuevas played on the Riviera, they were invited to produce their newest ballets in the garden at Yakymour for the delight of the Aga Khan and his guests. Television was bringing the screen into every home, but the Aga Khan was still rich enough, like the monarchs in the old days, to bring in the players.

I had met the Marquis de Cuevas earlier in London when he and his wife Marguerita, the favourite grand-daughter of John D. Rockefeller, invited me to dinner before we all went on to a reception at the Tate Gallery. The Marquis de Cuevas, who was born in Chile, was a pure delight, but as he never curbed his tongue he was always getting into trouble. He emitted a flow of brilliant ideas in an amazing Spanish accent. Marguerita, on this occasion, wore a black dress with a black chiffon mantilla and magnificent pearls and diamonds which made her look like a painting by Goya.

The Begum, when the marquis came to Yakymour,

quickly fell under his spell. 'He is *exquis*,' she said to me later. There was a story which delighted the Aga Khan. The marquis and the marquise often found themselves in different parts of America, or for that matter of the world. On this particular occasion Marguerita, who was in her New York home, had a tiff with her butler. When morning came she wanted her breakfast but she was not on speaking terms with the butler, so she telephoned to the marquis, who was in Palm Beach, asking him to get through to the butler on long distance and order her breakfast for her! That at least is how the story went.

Cannes . . . Paris . . . Assuan . . . Teheran. How could a princess with a husband such as the Aga Khan not be a romantic figure, especially when, as in the case of the Begum, she had known brown bread as well as white. Neither wealth nor position made her less naturally kind. When in 1949, while leaving Yakymour by car with the Aga Khan, she was ambushed by four armed bandits who stole jewels worth £160,000 from her, she thought only about the shock it might give her husband. 'Jewels are merely lent to us for a time,' she said to me later. 'The day always comes when one has to give them up.'

'I simply must show you my new hat!' she exclaimed. 'I bought it on the spur of the moment, just because I took a fancy to it. I mean that I did not choose it because I thought it would go well with any particular dress or suit —merely because I felt it would go with almost everything. Then again, I will tell you a secret. I mostly wear plain materials. I am a little suspicious of prints. I quickly become tired of a printed dress and I am sure that other people tire just as quickly of seeing us wear the same dress. However, I love blue and I succumbed at Geneviève Fath's the other day to this deep cornflower dress which you told me you liked. Note how wide the skirt is and how it crosses over, and that the top is really a close-fitting jacket! One should really call it a two-piece, I suppose. I like everything about it, the cotton, which is both stiff and supple, and the pocket on the hip in the form of a bow. The reason I am so pleased is that my hat might have been bought specially for it.'

Yes, indeed, her little hat was made up of tiny blue flowers faintly reminiscent of cornflowers against bright emerald leaves.

A darling hat, a magnificent dress, a real pearl necklace, and—a superb princess!

12

WE were almost on the eve of the Paris Grand Prix and I returned to the Avenue Marceau to call on Mme Suzy Volterra. The door of the apartment was opened cautiously. The maid exclaimed: 'Ah, it is you!' There was the sound of a chain being undone. The door opened wide and I went in.

I had, however, committed the unpardonable offence of calling on Mme Volterra without first warning her by telephone, but I think my instinct must have guided me because the maid added:

'Madame is in bed, but all the same I will tell her that you are here.'

She switched on all the lights in the drawing-room and left me alone for a few minutes, during which I had time to admire the cup for the 1955 Derby which stood on a low table. This famous cup reminded me of a story which Mme Volterra told me about the customs officer who asked her on her return to France after winning the race:

'Have you anything to declare, madame? Anything acquired abroad?'

'Nothing,' smiled Mme Volterra, 'except my coveted cup!'

'You have won a cup! What cup?'

'The cup for the Derby.'

'Well, if you have a cup and it was acquired abroad, I am afraid you will have to pay duty on it.'

'When I showed him the cup he admired it but was anxious to do his duty,' said Mme Volterra. 'I found it

rather comical, being received in this manner after winning
the Derby for France! Fortunately his superior put his
mind at rest, and I was allowed to bring in my cup without
paying duty on it.'

The maid returned saying:

'Madame is anxious to see you, so perhaps, if you are not
in too much of a hurry, you would wait?'

Of course I would wait, and clearly the maid was anxious
to gossip, for she continued:

'Do you not admire our flowers, mademoiselle?'

The drawing-room was full of deep red roses. There
were also hydrangeas but the roses predominated, roses of
high summer, superb and heavy with perfume. They had
been sent to her by the distinguished men who were her
guests at a dinner she had given the previous night at
Maxim's.

'You would not believe,' pursued the maid, 'how many
flowers I have arranged in my life. Fortunes in flowers
have passed through my hands. One needs a luxurious
home to provide an adequate setting for such flowers, and
a great deal of time to arrange them. Yesterday, for
instance, when these arrived I was glad to be alone.
Madame had gone to see her horses at Chantilly. I was
continually running to the door to receive fresh bouquets,
all of which had to be carefully unpacked and tastefully set
out in vases worthy of them. Yes, flowers need a great
deal of attention. One must constantly change the water,
for instance. That is important, you know, mademoiselle.'

Mademoiselle, alas, knew little about such luxury.
Mademoiselle sometimes received a dozen red roses for her
wedding anniversary or for her birthday, but mademoiselle
has never received so many flowers at one time. Mme
Volterra is madame. Mademoiselle is quite another
thing. To be mademoiselle in the eyes of a stylish lady's-
maid is not so much a symbol of youth as the precise

definition for a woman whose establishment is too modest
to be worthy of notice and who does not employ a lady's-
maid of her own—or even a cook or a chauffeur.
Mademoiselle is a negligible quantity, charming to gossip
with.   In short, she is a female journalist, a manicurist, or
the girl who brings hand-made lingerie!

'Yes,' the maid continued, 'I have certainly seen a great
many flowers, but if you would like me to tell you who has
sent most flowers in her life, and continues to do so, then it
is the beautiful actress Elvire Popesco.   Mme Popesco, it
would seem, is at her happiest when she is sending flowers
to her friends.   She spends astronomical figures on flowers.'

So Elvire Popesco, I reflected, that lovely Rumanian
butterfly, that incomparable artist, that heroine of the Paris
play *Tovaritch*, hovered from florist to florist!

Mme Volterra appeared in a *déshabillé* of cream satin.

'Forgive me!' she exclaimed.   'You cannot guess how
worried I am.   Oh no.   It was not my dinner at Maxim's.
That was a great success.   My dress was much admired.
The Aga Khan and his Begum remained till past one in the
morning.   As he had been late dressing, he told me how
from time to time he had looked in on the Begum, who
warned him that if he did not hurry she would not wait for
him.   "She carried out her threat," said the Aga Khan,
beaming.   "When I returned to kiss her she had flown!"'

She made me sit down beside her and went on:

'As soon as my last guest had disappeared I drove back
here, changed from my beautiful evening dress into tweeds,
and drove to Chantilly.   To-day I have my dress for the
Grand Prix to try on.   I have not a moment and I am
worried because, with the Grand Prix almost on us, I am
not yet certain whether my jockey will be able to ride
Phil Drake.   Another owner claims to have engaged
him for the race.   I am anxiously waiting for a telephone
call to clear up the muddle.'

I had heard of women such as the Marquise de Cuevas having troubles with a butler, others having anxious moments about a maid or even a charwoman, but never before with—a jockey! In spite of all the affection that I had for Mme Volterra, I found it difficult to see myself in such a state of anxiety. And yet, I reflected, it was not generous of me to remain so unmoved by what to her was a matter of immense importance. My eyes kept roving round the room, from the red roses that filled the air with perfume to the thick carpet which is a dream to walk on, one's high heels sinking into the wool; from the beautiful curtains which frame glimpses of the Arc de Triomphe outside to the pictures on the walls; from the red silk settee on which we were both seated to Mme Volterra's satin *déshabillé* worthy of a queen or an empress.

'If my husband were here,' said Mme Volterra suddenly, 'I would probably be playing cards with him. Playing cards was a passion with him and I am sorry that he died before canasta was invented. He would have delighted in it.'

After the Grand Prix, after Ascot, she would go and spend a few weeks in the south of France.

'I am tired,' she confessed. 'I need a long rest. I have lost weight, and as I have not attempted to slim it is clear that I am living on my nerves. I must do some fishing—that, at least, is a soothing pastime.'

She bade me farewell, telling me that I had merely to let her know if I decided to go to the Grand Prix, but she added that it was a race for which she had no love—a hard race with too many horses, too much noise. However, the Grand Prix was the Grand Prix, and she really must try on her dress.

'Talking of dresses, when I went to London I only took one evening dress, not even expecting to wear it, but I won the Derby and I found myself committed to three important evenings—my own party, that of Lord Willoughby de Broke, and one to celebrate the elections—and I was obliged to wear the same dress on all three occasions. Imagine how I felt about it when I had cupboards packed with dresses both here, at my Paris apartment, and at Chantilly! However, I expect it was that modest little dress which helped to bring me my good fortune.'

She took me to the door and bade me an affectionate farewell. As I hurried away I heard the chain being put back into place. The beautiful widow was back in her nest—and in front of me in all its glory was the Arc de Triomphe!

13

I SET out one morning for the Rue Jacob, a narrow, picturesque street of antique furniture dealers, publishers, and small old-world hotels on the left bank of the Seine. Yvonne de Rothschild—Mrs Anthony de Rothschild—had said to me before I left London: 'Go and see my sister, Renée de Monbrison, in her little shop.'

I had already met her, though rather briefly, at a family gathering at Wing, but I had spent most of the time talking to her mother, Mme Sonia Cahen d'Anvers, by the fire in the big drawing-room, while Yvonne's daughter, another Renée—Renée de Rothschild—in a magnificent bridal gown stood by the window beside the blond young man she had just married, Mr Peter Robeson, the international show jumper. As they stood shaking hands with their guests Renée's favourite dog lay obediently behind them, and the whole picture was evocative of the formality and dignity of a more leisurely age.

Sonia Cahen d'Anvers was happiness itself on this occasion, and how indeed could she be otherwise on this beautiful grand-daughter's wedding day! Her own daughters, the London one and the Paris one, were momentarily under the same roof, the roof of this lovely Rothschild home. Physically they were much alike—the same voice, the same gestures, the same bright eyes—but I remembered thinking at the time that whereas Yvonne's eyes sought one out like searchlights and held one in their grip, Renée de Monbrison's eyes were softer and less insistent. The effect of light-coloured eyes in dark-haired women is very striking.

'Renée de Monbrison, my Paris daughter,' Mme d'Anvers was saying to me, 'is the essence of unselfishness, eternally ready to be of help, and though I am nearly eighty I find myself being continually surprised by her limitless goodness.'

There she was, this Paris daughter, on the other side of a table on which stood a bowl of roses! Tall, slim, and very elegant, her every movement was full of grace. She would suddenly sit on the arm of a chair as if it were a throne. She spoke in quick, warm tones, and was surrounded by her family from France, her daughter Françoise, her son-in-law, and their children.

There was a suggestion of royalty in these visiting families, relatives accustomed to seeking one another out, calling upon one another, half across Europe. The women had the gift of tongues, and spoke a great number without accent as did educated women in the past, when it was not the fashion to send girls to college or university but to educate them at home in purely feminine accomplishments.

On arriving at the Rue Jacob I did not immediately succeed in finding Renée's shop. I had forgotten the number, but Yvonne had told me that her sister had a passion for making lamps out of divers objects of historical value. Half way down this medieval street I came upon it, a window with RENÉE D'ANVERS written over it, a cobbled gateway leading into a succession of seventeenth-century houses and cool, unexpected gardens. The shop was entered through the gateway by a little fairy-tale door, and behind a yellow curtain, drawn across a corner to make a minute office, stood Renée with a telephone receiver to her ear.

'Come in!' she exclaimed. 'Yvonne told me that you would come. Find a chair to sit on.'

I sat very gingerly on the edge of a Louis Philippe satin-covered chair bearing a price tag, my hand-bag on my lap, my feet close together. Renée carried on with her telephonic conversation, and I heard her say:

'Yes, the poor dear man is dead at last. He suffered frightfully, I fear. The drugs ceased to act. Ah, but I have sensational news for you! She has just had a baby boy, and I am told that it is the most beautiful baby in all the world! Well, I must be leaving you. You will be glad to hear that Françoise's child is out of danger. The fever has subsided. Good-bye and a big kiss!'

Like a tragic actress, Renée emerged from behind her curtain.

'There!' she cried. 'You have just heard the day's news so far—the death of a very dear friend, the birth of a baby, and the fact that my two-year-old grandson developed acute appendicitis and almost died. I have been terribly anxious these last few hours.'

I was still seated on the edge of the pretty lemon-coloured arm-chair but I had time to look about me. The portico through which I came must have been the entrance to a stately town house in the days when one drove through cobbled streets in a lumbering coach and when one's husband wore lace cuffs and a plumed hat! The house and its annexes now accommodated, in addition to Renée, several other antique dealers. In stone cellars more than seven hundred years old, that once formed part of a subterranean passage leading to the Abbaye de St-Germain-des-Prés, there was, according to a painted sign, a picturesque restaurant with an old-fashioned spit.

Renée's shop was crowded with pretty tables on which stood innumerable artistic objects. Through a wide expanse of glass one looked upward at the people walking

F

in the street, and I was surprised to see how many of them stopped to inspect and comment on the treasures set out for their delight. Yvonne was right. Her sister must have a passion for lamps, and as I am a practical woman I was very taken with these transformations which turned the pretty oil lamps of our grandmothers' youthful days into charming electric lamps for modern apartments. Yes, these reconditioned old lamps were adorable. Their chief value was that they were once to be found in very modest homes. This tall one, for instance, with the topaz globe was strikingly evocative of the white linen-aproned servant with her long hair done up in a bun, who at dusk could come into her mistress's boudoir holding this precious object already warmly alive with an orange light.

What I liked also about these objects of fifty years ago or more was that they give one the illusion of feeling, by comparison, so very young! How many times had this lemon-coloured arm-chair on which I was sitting been bought and sold? I suspected, indeed I had no doubt, that some young woman entering the shop would very soon fall in love with it and carry it away. How fortunate to remain for so long agreeable to the eye, so that strangers continue to fall in love with you!

'Antique dealers,' said Renée reflectively, 'have an important role to play in a world in which most modern apartments look like hospital wards. Many people, I think, are beginning to feel conscious of a void in their lives, and in an effort to remedy it they plunge into the first antique dealer's they see. Do some of these objects, for instance, strike you as naïvely provincial? Well, that is just what is needed to soften the effects of glaring white walls. They bring a family atmosphere into the home.'

I asked her where she discovered these things, and she told me that the pretty cherry-wood table beside me came from the Marché aux Puces. 'I was fortunate,' she said. 'The table is very fine.' Yes, indeed, but was she not brought up with her sister at Champs, one of the most historic castles in France? In those surroundings one would surely imbibe beauty from earliest girlhood! Nearer the window were several pieces of Worcester china, and why had she chosen these English table mats so dear to Victorian hostesses? 'They are very popular in France,' she explained. 'The French clamour for what is English just as what is French has a romantic appeal in England.'

By an association of ideas she said suddenly:

'The lovely house of which this forms a part once housed a British ambassador, and for this reason is known as the Hôtel d'Angleterre. The portico must certainly have seen many a sedan chair pass through it. I think also that the Maréchal de Saxe lived here during the reign of Louis XV.

'I have a colleague who some time ago bought a great collection of coloured glass balloons such as people used to hang over arbours in the days of Guy de Maupassant. You will now find them hanging in fine profusion at the entrance to the first little garden. Who collected them and why? That is the charm of this business. The gardens with their wild grass and little shrubs are themselves full of statues. If you are not bitten, at some time in your life, by the collector's bug there must be something wrong with you. The trouble is that we who sell antiques cannot know what each passer-by collects, for if we could discover this, and anticipate his coming, our task would be relatively simple.

'For instance, a very famous woman whom we both know was telling me the other day that she walks out of her Paris house every Friday morning with ten thousand francs in her bag to spend at antique shops.'

14

'IT would be a trite thing to say that in the antique business one is always learning something new and strange,' said Mme Renée de Monbrison, 'but do you know, for instance, what a "little house of crime" is? An Englishwoman told me. She came here and picked up a tiny porcelain house that I had brought over from London. I had paid very little for it but I thought it pretty.

'"This," said my customer, "is what is known as a 'little house of crime,' the model of a house in which a murder has taken place. Unfortunately this one is not marked. The murderer's name is not written on it. That, from the collector's point of view, renders it less valuable."

'I have not sold my "little house of crime,"' Renée continued. 'The important point is that I have learned what to look out for. As soon as a customer comes in and I am able to explain to her the meaning of an object, I am half way to selling it. Now, suppose you come and have lunch with me?'

At lunch we talked about our families. We are women with two countries, France and England. We stand up for the French when we are in England, and for the English when we are in France. Occasionally we feel that women who are entirely one or the other are more fortunate than we are. What pitfalls and complications they avoid! On the other hand, do they live as intensely as Renée and I?

Two countries, two languages: what wide, exciting windows!

We went back to the shop. Renée had brought a big basket of flowers and these she proceeded to dispose artistically about the place. Her expression was thoughtful. I watched her putting two or three marigolds in a tumbler.

'These tumblers,' she said, 'are known as wedding tumblers—*verres de mariage*. They were used at country weddings fifty years ago and were not considered at all valuable, but as everything in those days was well made, to-day they are greatly sought after by collectors.'

Renée placed the tumbler with the marigolds beside a lamp. I was amused to see her so deftly arranging a drawing-room for the benefit of strangers passing in the street. She took up two yellow rosebuds, that looked as if they were made of porcelain, and found a vase for them. She then cut the stems of half a dozen wild carnations, the sort that grow in English borders or beside mountain streams. She dusted a little, and when she had finished this housework came to sit down beside me.

'This was a tiny grocer's shop,' she began, with that sudden change of subject which is characteristic of our sex. 'A woman friend advised me to start a small business. This friend said: "You should begin with lamps. One always has such trouble in finding them, and one needs so many, not only for oneself but as wedding presents." I liked the idea. Pretty things attract me, but I admit that when I was a girl I scarcely gave a thought to the beautiful things in our home. I suppose I took them for granted. At all events, my friend and I began looking out for a suitable shop. I wanted to be on the left bank and we haunted the Rue Bonaparte, the Rue Furstemberg, and the Rue Jacob. I quite lost my heart to the little grocer's shop into which one walked through the portico of this noble house.

'The woman behind the counter was in deep mourning.

The grocer, her husband, had just died, and the responsibilities of managing the place weighed on her shoulders.
We had little difficulty in persuading her to sell out,
especially when we told her that we ourselves had no
intention of setting up as grocers!

'I loved moving in, and because the money came from
my father I painted my maiden name, Renée d'Anvers,
outside. Finding lamps was an easy matter, and I discovered two people who made exquisite lampshades. A
lovely lampshade is like a hat signed by a famous Paris
modiste: the hat enhances the beauty of the wearer, the
lampshade enhances the beauty of the lamp. An ugly
shade will ruin a lamp, even if the lamp itself is priceless.'

How charming to be seated with her in this pretty room
overlooking the grey, narrow houses in the Rue Jacob! At
three Mme Cahen d'Anvers arrived, smiling and fresh as a
rose. She almost danced between the furniture as she
described in her delightful Russian accent her lunch amongst
students in the Latin Quarter. Her plans for the evening
were already made. She had a concert at which there was
to be music by Dvořák. Lightly she drew aside the
curtain to telephone to a friend in Russian, but a moment
later was back with us, asking her daughter:

'Have you sold anything to-day, *ma chérie?*'

'No, Mother. Nothing yet.'

'Oh, my darling. How very sad!'

'Not sad, Mother, *voyons!* Not in the least sad!'

Renée picked up a tin of beeswax and started with long,
slow strokes to polish the cherry-wood table. In a few
moments the pretty wood shone like an autumn chestnut,
and a lovely smell filled the room.

'I love this table,' Renée declared. 'I shall, of course,
be glad to sell it, but what a void it will leave! Besides,
my English table mats look so nice on it. I am unhappy
enough to be losing that picture on the wall.'

'Have you sold a picture then?' asked Mme Cahen d'Anvers.

'Yes, but it was not my picture. A dealer lent it to me. However, a charming gentleman stopped to look at some Worcester porcelain through the window. I had just put on display part of a set which I was busy washing. He came in and asked to see a plate that I was drying. I handed it to him. I was so afraid to miss a sale! He examined some other things, and then suddenly saw this picture and fell in love with it. He told me that he came from the Pyrenees, and as my husband, like Cyrano de Bergerac, is a Gascon, and I know every inch of the country as far as Bordeaux, we met on common ground. He turned out to be a nobleman and now he writes me long letters in exquisite old-fashioned French. When next he comes to Paris he will take the picture away with him.'

Two young Italian boys, after peering through the window, their noses flattened against the pane, came in to inquire the price of a tiny mandoline in mother-of-pearl. Renée consulted an exercise book in which she kept such information, the top price and the bottom price, she explained. The Italians were quite beautiful to look at and their shirts were soft and elegant, while their wide-shouldered tweed jackets hung with that loose abandon which was the latest male fashion. We listened while they talked Italian. They adored the mandoline but . . . 'Madame, we cannot quite afford it. Our holidays are almost at an end and we have very little money left.'

'That is a pity for both you and me,' said Renée implacably. 'You should have come earlier.'

Mme Cahen d'Anvers, meanwhile, was again on the telephone talking to a Russian friend. The Italians took their leave and Mme d'Anvers put down the receiver.

'What!' she cried. 'Do you mean to tell me that they gave you all that trouble without buying anything?'

'Maman! maman!' answered her daughter. 'Have I
not told you a thousand times that one needs a great deal
of patience in this business!'

A woman came into the shop to inquire if Renée would
like to buy a Napoleonic bed in perfect condition.

'Alas!' answered Renée. 'I would not know where to
put it. My shop is far too small. I specialize in little
things for people to take away.'

'Then can you tell me, madame, who would like to buy
a Napoleonic bed?'

'You need merely inquire up and down the street. I
would be surprised if you did not quickly find a purchaser.
The Rue Jacob is a ladder on each rung of which is an old
curiosity shop.'

The little woman thanked us and walked off. Mme
d'Anvers declared that she also must be going. She had
promised to call on her Russian friend, though she was not
certain about how to get there.

'Renée, my dear, you must tell me which omnibus I
should take. I am sure there must be an omnibus.'

'Yes, Mother, there is, but you would need to walk quite
a way to catch it. Stay with us ten minutes longer and I
will find you a cab.'

We plunged back into family gossip, but after a while
Mme d'Anvers opened her hand-bag and exclaimed:

'You must both of you help me to choose some material
for a new dress!'

She laid out the various patterns on her lap, and our
three heads bent eagerly over them. Mme d'Anvers
favoured the grey material, but Renée and I cried out:

'Oh no, not the grey one! It is far too old for you!'

Mme d'Anvers looked up at us with an indulgent smile:

'But I *am* an old lady!'

Then suddenly, in a different voice:

'You have not told me, Renée, how you like my hat. I

have discovered a modiste, a real pearl, and she brings her models to my apartment so that my friend and I can try them all on. We enjoy ourselves immensely!'

Grandmothers, indeed, are very gay. Their age allows them to assume the role of spectator in this turbulent world. They sympathize with our sorrows without allowing their hearts to be too seriously torn as ours, the hearts of younger women, too often are.

Renée ran out into the street and hailed a cab.

A young woman with large brown eyes arrived, beautiful eyes though sad. She smoked furiously while recounting the latest news about Renée's little grandson. He was much better but she was vexed by his naughtiness. Yesterday he was dying. To-day he was saved, but was very naughty! The two women went on to talk about the death of a very good friend and the birth of another baby. I had heard these events discussed from so many angles that I had developed what amounted to a family interest in them.

The young woman then changed the subject to women's magazines. Expertly she dissected the latest numbers of *Elle* and *Marie Claire*. Of a short story she said:

'I liked it very much because the illustration was so pretty!'

As I myself was an avid reader of women's magazines, and of these two in particular, I listened intently to what she had to say, and I quickly discovered that though she worked in a laboratory, her three brothers with whom she lived were all artists. No wonder she was more interested in the illustration than in the story! With an ease that filled me with admiration she turned from art to science, and I gathered that she knew a great deal about isotopes, creosotes, and cultures.

These technical terms escaped from her pretty, painted

lips as if they were words in everyday use. I tried to assess the impact that so much knowledge had made on this young woman of twenty-five, who was still unmarried. She told me that she was very tired. Could this be the reason, I wondered, for that touch of sadness that haunted her beautiful brown eyes? Is it wise for us women to cram too much study into our early years?

A woman passing along the narrow street, having caught sight of the cherry-wood table, came into the shop to inquire the price of it, whereupon Renée, removing the lamps and table mats, explained how the table could be extended. Did this require much effort, the woman wanted to know.

'No, madame,' answered Renée. 'See how easy it is to handle! That in itself proves the excellent workmanship of the days when it was made.'

When Renée expressed an opinion, I had the curious feeling that it was almost more for her own benefit than for the customer's. She seemed quietly to state truths learned from childhood. She added leaves to the table, then removed one of them so that we looked down upon a half-moon. Renée's movements were smooth, unhurried, and caressing. The customer, busy picturing the table in her own dining-room, asked:

'Would it seat twelve to dinner?'

'Yes, if the twelve were willing to sit rather close to one another. Ten, on the other hand, would manage very comfortably. But do you often sit twelve?'

The customer seemed taken aback by this question, but the table pleased her and, like a little girl touching a much-desired doll, she placed a finger gently on the shiny surface.

'I have not had it long enough to give it all the polishing it needs,' said Renée, 'but the wood is superb.'

The customer decided to think about it and apologized to Renée for giving so much trouble.

'That is what I am here for,' answered Renée.

When we were alone Renée exclaimed, laughing:

'How fortunate that Mother is with her Russian friend! She is so vexed when a customer goes away without buying anything!'

A delicious smell of roast chicken reached us from the subterranean passage that in former days led to the Abbaye de St-Germain-des-Prés. A man unrolled a long red carpet from the street to the restaurant and then flanked it with tubs of flowers. The night-club was preparing to open!

'When I am alone in the evening,' said Renée, 'that is to say when I am not needed by any member of my family, I remain in the shop until it is very late. All these gay folk arriving for dinner in the restaurant downstairs amuse me. One night I invited a party of people who were waiting for a table to come in. There was a miniature chest of drawers, a lovely little thing with a rounded front, that had been mine since girlhood. I was so accustomed to seeing it that I scarcely noticed it any more. One of the men in the party went straight up to it. Another did the same. They asked me the price and I answered them almost curtly, because I was in conversation with the women and I had asked these people in as friends, not as customers.

'"Well," said one man to the other, "if you do not want to buy this thing, I will."

'He bought it, and while they were having supper I packed it carefully so that it was ready for them when they called for it. Thus for me the evening proved both pleasant and profitable.

'To-day I have not made a single sale. Let us close the shop early. I must call at the hospital to see my grandson, after which you will come home with me and we shall have dinner together.'

The young woman with the beautiful eyes emptied the

ash-tray she had quietly been filling with cigarette stubs and ash. Renée arranged the cushions in the arm-chairs, extinguished some of the lamps and lit others. The shop was about to enter upon its nightly vigil. The lamps Renée lit shed a soft, warm glow over the Worcester china and the oil-painting on the wall which the nobleman from the Pyrenees would soon be calling for.

We locked the glass door, hailed a taxi, and drove to hospital.

When Renée rejoined me at the end of her visit she told me that her grandson was much better.

'His parents should be able to sleep to-night,' she added with relief.

Renée's apartment was on the ground floor in the Rue de Varenne, and as soon as the door opened her cat, looking very weird, rushed towards us and began to purr. The animal had not been well, and to prevent it from scratching Renée had tied an indiarubber balloon round its neck, with the result that it looked like a prehistoric beast; but it was the most playful cat in the world, and was wild with delight at the sight of its mistress.

A young woman architect who had a studio in the building came down to join us. Though we were three career women most of our conversation turned on our families. The young architect told me that she had two sons at school in England, and when during the course of my visit she called up a friend on the telephone, there followed a long discussion about Mediterranean cruises, and coach tours in distant countries. People have never travelled so far for their holidays, and those of us who own houses in the country appear terribly old-fashioned. How many women would consent to-day to spend their vacations year after year in the same place?

But Renée and I were happy to do so. She dreamed of going to her house near Arcachon with Mick, her cat, wearing its fantastic dandy's ruff, and at Arcachon she would wait patiently for her children, and her grandchildren, and all their friends who would arrive with or without warning as fancy took them. They would certainly retail their troubles and their dreams and she, while arranging flowers in tiny vases or transforming an old Chinese teapot, the lid of which had been lost or cracked, into a sweetly pretty lamp, would listen sympathetically.

While we were at supper the father of the baby boy arrived to ask his mother-in-law if she would look in at the hospital because the baby was to have an injection. Its mother was so very tired, he explained.

'Of course,' answered Renée, 'and on my way home I will call on my daughter to kiss her and to reassure her. I am so very fortunate to live on the ground floor. I am in the street in no time.'

This woman, I reflected, as I gazed with affectionate admiration upon Renée, had been in the course of one day antique dealer, housewife, cook, respectful and attentive daughter, warm friend to the young woman with the sad-looking eyes, loving mother, and tender granny to her ailing grandson. What a superb tribute to womanhood!

15

I SPENT a quiet morning walking aimlessly through the streets behind the Madeleine. After a while I went up to an *agent de ville* and said to him:

'*Monsieur l'agent*, can you direct me to the Chapelle Expiatoire?'

What had given me a sudden urge to visit this chapel, built by Louis XVIII in the cemetery of the Madeleine as an act of atonement to the memory of his brother, the martyred Louis XVI, and of Marie Antoinette?

The *agent de ville* was directing traffic in the middle of the Boulevard Haussmann, but there was not a great deal of it because it was Monday, and the two loveliest department stores, the Printemps and the Galeries Lafayette, slept like two gilded cocoons. I sensed that the *agent de ville* on his island site was mostly listening for the offending horn, because in Paris at that time there was a great drive against noise. What was once the noisiest capital in the world was now the quietest. Only fire-engines and ambulances might break the rule. The motorist who rashly sounded his horn was fined. What an excellent law! No longer as I crossed the street did male drivers, coming up unexpectedly, frighten the life out of me with their klaxons merely for the fun of seeing a woman jump!

The *agent de ville* looked at me and answered:

'That, madame, is one of the sights of Paris that I do not need to look up in my little book.'

Very gallantly he pointed out the way.

I entered a tiny garden in which children were playing and where young women, wearing ballerina shoes and cotton dresses, bent their graceful heads over school books.

Examinations were beginning. The lodge keeper led me to the chapel. On this beautiful sunny morning the lawns, dotted with rose-trees, isolated us from the bustle of the city. The scene was evocative of some picturesque corner in a provincial town.

The chapel was open and in it, exquisitely carved in marble, a figure of Louis XVI with an angel whose features were those of the Abbé Edgeworth, an Irish priest, who is said to have attended the king on the guillotine, and called out to him as the knife was about to fall: 'Son of St Louis, ascend to heaven!' At the foot of the statue I read tender, human words composed by the king in prison which represented his last testament.

I then turned with still deeper emotion to the figure of Marie Antoinette accompanied by the angel of religion. The lovely, unhappy queen also had a page engraved at the base of her statue. How nobly and with what magnificent feminine courage did this woman, accused by so many of vanity and extravagance, meet death!

Louis XVI and Marie Antoinette, their decapitated heads between their legs, were laid here after execution and covered with lime. Later their remains were transferred to St Denis.

Two pretty lawns gay with rose-trees, which at first reminded me of a lawyer's garden in some small French town, mark the site of two deep trenches into which were thrown 1,300 victims of the guillotine, as well as 500 Swiss Guards who fell defending the Tuileries in 1792. Here also were buried Charlotte Corday, who assassinated Marat in his bath, the chemist Lavoisier, and Mme Elizabeth, tender sister of Louis XVI, who was to prove one of Marie Antoinette's last companions.

The chirruping of birds mingled with the cries of children, one of whom had just fallen on a gravel path and cut her knee. When I emerged into the traffic of the Boulevard Haussman, it was with dimmed eyes.

16

WALKING along the Boulevard Mals-
herbes, I suddenly caught sight of the
name: Anny Blatt.

To any woman who knits as much as I
do, this name was certain to spell magic.
Knitting is my passion. In the immense number of garments that I have made and then unpicked, either to save
money or merely because of my natural respect for wool in
all its forms and colours, I must even have surpassed the
record of Homer's heroine Penelope, wife of Ulysses. As
I never knit from a pattern but allow my imagination to
guide me, I have invented scores of designs, some of which
I have had the satisfaction of seeing copied and launched
into fashion. I am not entirely surprised when this
happens. Like the poet André Chenier who put his hand
to his heart, crying out 'I had something here!' I undoubtedly had something with my knitting-needles and
my wool. To enable me to read while knitting, my
designs are extremely simple. Every book I read, whether
romantic or serious, has produced its garment. This
method prevents me from skipping, because to skip a
paragraph would strike me in the same way as to drop a
stitch. I take a pride in my work.

Well, here I was on this lovely morning in front of the
establishment of the Queen of Knitting. She has risen to
heights I cannot attain, for though on occasion I have sold
my prose, I have never been able to sell a piece of knitting.

My mind suddenly made up, I very deliberately entered
the stronghold. My favourite London store often displays
a picture of Anny Blatt against mountains of wool in
adorable colours—colours that make one dream. Are we

ever sufficiently grateful for the joy we obtain from vivid colours?

I lightly climbed the stairs leading to the *salon*. There were white chairs with brown, yellow, and russet-coloured cushions, and through open windows I could see the tops of the trees in the boulevard. After sending my name in to Mme Anny Blatt, I settled down comfortably to watch a number of elegant women trying on cardigans in pastel shades. Some of them were tanned by the sun and I pictured them as spending holidays by sea or mountain; others I saw picking flowers, watching over a sleeping baby, making jam in a gleaming copper pan.

'If madame will come this way . . .'

A young woman led me to Mme Anny Blatt who was seated behind an imposing table. She was blonde with streaks of gold, tiny of stature, and dressed in a sapphire blue suit. Vigorous, animated hands flashed out a charming welcome, and without wasting a moment she exclaimed:

'I have sent for two girls to put on some knitted things so that while we are talking you will have a clear picture of my work.'

When the first model appeared in a hand-knitted suit, Mme Blatt explained why it was that these suits each took a month to make.

'Did you ever as a little girl read a fairy story about a beautiful princess being locked up in a high tower by a witch and being given seemingly impossible tasks to do?' she asked. 'These hand-knitted suits are feats of infinite patience. The knitting which the women do is mounted on stiff, fine tulle so that it resembles tweed, and can then be cut out with scissors like a material. Suits of this kind never look home-made, though that is precisely what they are! Do not imagine, however, that I despise the ordinary pullover that every woman makes in her spare time. On the contrary. There are not enough to go round.'

G

Her eyes suddenly turned to the mannequin:

'Mademoiselle,' she said curtly, 'there is a stain on your suit!'

The mannequin blushingly explained that the accident had only just happened but that she would immediately have it removed. A few moments later she came back wearing a suit knitted not by hand this time but by machine —and I was shown several of these in different colours.

'What I like best is their simplicity!' I said to Mme Blatt.

'They *must* be simple,' she answered. 'Knitting is a most wonderful art. Though it has been known for centuries, we are often inclined to regard it as being quite a new invention. This is because, during recent years, it has become extremely popular with both sexes in every class of society. Mother, father, all the children have their cardigans and pullovers. What a saving! What an insurance against a sudden chill! What else is there as useful that every housewife has learned to make, almost by instinct, since girlhood!'

'Your name, Mme Blatt, has become synonymous with knitting. Are you a keen knitter? Do you between conferences, on your way to and from London and New York, stretch out a hand for your knitting basket?'

'No,' she answered, laughing, 'I do not. Let me confess it right away. Knitting as a mere pastime would not have been enough to bring me to my present position. I was born at Mulhouse in the heart of the textile industry and my father was a weaver. My husband was in textiles. I know almost everything there is to be known about weaving and spinning. I have probed the secrets of every thread and yarn. The various nylons are as familiar to me as cotton, and all the new fibres, just as soon as they are invented, quickly become my friends. I never allow myself likes or dislikes. Comparisons are a waste of time. There is only one test of a new yarn and that is its usefulness.

'Prettiness, of course, is a delightful and necessary adjunct. When I was a girl all the women round me knitted—those in my own family, the maids, the goose girls, and the nuns in my convent; but I was shocked by the fact that the garments they knitted were so coarse. I felt angry that such a precious art should be put to such bad use.

'In America I have been described as a genius. That is nonsense. Far too many people are credited with genius these days. I may, however, lay claim to working ferociously hard. I work every single moment of the day. As soon as a woman in business begins going to cocktail-parties, she is half way to failure.

'My parents brought me up under an iron discipline. They never overlooked even the slightest sign of disobedience, and yet I was tenderly loved and the happiest little girl in the world. At the convent to which they sent me the discipline was no less strict, but when I came out into the marriage market I had all the accomplishments then considered necessary for a young woman. The nuns taught me never to waste a moment. That is the greatest safeguard that any woman can have against the threat of boredom.

'I have a passion for air travel. When I know that a long business journey is imperative, I always go by air. In this way I have an impression that I am cheating time. Instead of wasting it, I catch up on it. Apart from this, I enjoy being in an aeroplane, and if I were eighteen I would be tempted to become an air hostess! I own a country estate near Orly, and every time I hear an aeroplane I put my head out of the window to catch a glimpse of it, or if I am in the garden I gaze upwards as full of wonderment as any child.

'Seriously, however, if I were eighteen I would try to build up the same sort of business as I have now. This is a wonderful age for women to climb to the top. Let ambitious girls take encouragement from me, for all this great undertaking is to-day my own, from the drawer of my desk to the electric lamps that hang from the ceiling.

'My husband was involved in one of the most sensational crashes in the history of the cotton industry. He was an amazing man, but he would never take feminine advice. I continually said of the textiles he showed me: "I would not buy that print if I saw it in a shop. I just do not think it pretty." He would give me a pitying look, the look of a man who thinks that a woman should not meddle in business—that she should confine herself to running the home and providing small talk at dinner-parties—and he would cut me short brutally, like a person slamming a book closed.

'I used to be terribly hurt, but disciplined as I had been, I accepted it. Discipline, however, though making one obey does not prevent one from thinking what one would do if one were in charge. Then suddenly my husband's business crashed.

'From being one of the wealthiest, one of the most spoiled women in the whole of France, I became one of the poorest. Everything I possessed was sold. Thus I arrived one day in Paris with my little girl, Anny, penniless and looking for work.

'Oh, the back stairs that I went up and down, the heat of a Paris summer under burning attic slates, the cold in winter! When my husband met me struggling under two heavy suit-cases full of knitted garments that I was trying to sell, he would exclaim:

'"How can you make such an exhibition of yourself?"

'He hated the idea that I, a woman, should try to regain our fortune. Soon after this he died, and then you may be sure that I was more than ever grateful for that hard Alsatian training. I made full use of it. I felt certain that I had something worth while in me, and then again—there was my daughter, in whose eyes, each time she looked up at me, there was such utter confidence.

'I took an attic in the Faubourg St-Honoré with two women friends, and was able to persuade an American firm to give me an order for some pullovers. We produced them—very pretty ones—delivered them on the agreed day, received another order, then another, until from these beginnings I found myself at the head of a business. Saleswomanship is a gift, and I have it in a high degree because I believe implicitly in everything that I sell. My daughter Anny has grown up to be an adorable partner. She it was who brought you in just now.'

The young woman who brought me to her mother gave no clue to her being the daughter of the house. I had noticed, however, that she spoke to Mme Blatt with tender respect.

The two mannequins were still busy showing us knitted dresses, and I reflected that duchess or typist would look equally nice in them. They were just what one would love to wear—tailored collars, sober, harmonious buttoning, and pockets which curved gracefully with the hips. I liked particularly one in navy blue and another in pink.

Mme Blatt, whose eyes missed nothing, said firmly to one of the girls:

'I don't like your hair style, mademoiselle. It contributes neither to your personality nor to your looks. Did you go to a local hairdresser?'

'Oh no, madame,' answered the girl, looking distressed. 'I had it done by Monsieur X himself.'

She mentioned one of the most famous hairdressers in Paris.

'Well,' retorted Mme Blatt, 'he has not shown himself capable of doing you justice, and I am afraid that you will have to go to an even more famous hairdresser than the famous Monsieur X. See to it that your hair style is changed for the next collection. You must learn to bring out your personality.'

Turning to me she asked:

'How do you like the dresses, Mme Henrey?'

'If I were rich enough I would order a dozen!' I answered, laughing.

'That is exactly what American women do,' she cried. 'They order a whole range of dresses and cardigans in different colours. When I first started in business, it used to be said that the very wearability of knitted goods would limit the demand, but of course it was just the opposite. When a woman feels herself at ease in a dress or a pullover, she immediately wants to own more in different colours. I gambled on this, and I brought down prices to such an extent that to-day a woman can buy five knitted dresses for the same money as a single dress would have cost her a few years ago.

'Women love to wear different colours, but we must help them to satisfy this urge without putting them in a position where they must continually ask their husbands for money. Career girls also must keep an eye on their spending. Typists, shop-girls, secretaries, actresses, singers, need to make their pay packets go as far as possible.

'People from all over the world come to ask me how to adapt these new fibres that are continually being discovered. We are only on the fringe of such inventions, and the curious thing is that not one of them, however popular it becomes, ever entirely displaces those that came before!'

'Do you think, Mme Blatt, that women will soon cease to knit by hand?'

'On the contrary,' she cried. 'Women to-day in spite of having less time at their disposal continue to knit a great deal by hand. I have stands for knitting wool both at the Printemps and at the Galeries Lafayette where very pretty models can be examined by customers, and these are always in demand.'

'But consider all the women who made lace until a few

years ago! Now, even in the Auvergne, one hardly ever sees a woman making it. Soon the art will have become extinct.'

'That is true,' answered Mme Blatt. 'But lace, though a beautiful luxury, was never essential. The upkeep also required cleverness and patience. Women no longer wash and iron as our grandmothers used to. Even in Paris the ironing woman is losing her skill. Knitting is quite a different story. Even a beginner can make something useful with her needles. She can knit a wool cap for her little girl while listening to the band playing in the park. What she knits is youthful, elegant, warm, cheap, and fresh as a daisy. There is no upkeep to it at all. When she is tired of her little girl's bonnet she can unpick it, wash the wool, and start making something quite different, a pair of gloves, for example. Nothing gives the average woman so much satisfaction as knowing how to knit, because it combines amusement with usefulness!'

'Have you any colour that you have made your own— like Schiaparelli with her shocking pink or Mme Agnès with her Agnès blue?'

'No, I have made a friend of every colour. I love them all. I guard myself against prejudices. I study what women like in every country. I speak three languages faultlessly—French, English, and German—and I read everything I can in these languages. I have just completed my fifty-seventh round trip to New York, and American women buy three hundred knitted dresses from me every day! I am constantly in England also, and many of my prettiest designs are made at Leicester, in which city only the other day I discovered an old loom which I have adapted to produce quite a sensational new design. One must think young, see young, so as to bear the requirements of the young in mind.'

'Tell me about yourself—the things you enjoy.'

'I am happier in a woollen coat, if it is properly cut, than in mink. I love jewels, but a burglar stole mine the other day, and in order to get at them smashed some lovely furniture. I hate night-clubs, and prefer the cinema to the theatre. I have seen innumerable plays, but a good film is like a short trip abroad. Music I adore, but as I seldom have time to go to a concert I play Beethoven on the gramophone, which leaves me free to work as I listen. Doing two things at once is another way of cheating time! One of the reasons I live outside Paris is for the exhilaration of driving to work in the morning and home at night. I like to see the panorama of people, streets, houses, and trees unfold before me, but what I like best—doubtless traceable to my Alsatian heritage—is to go up a mountain in search of Alpine flowers. What could be more romantic than looking for a tiny flower on a large mountain! Since I arrived penniless in Paris I have never taken more than one week's holiday a year. Work is like a jet aeroplane. The faster you work, the more work you find to do. Ideas come the same way. I am never at a loss for an idea. One idea is the spark for another, but it is essential to ensure that your ideas are a faithful reflection of yourself. For example, I am not at all happy with draped or flared dresses. For me the sheath silhouette always!'

'Do you slim to keep your own line?'

'Not exactly, but my daughter and I lunch every day on fresh fruit and ideas! I find that it is during the lunch-hour, while my employees are in the canteen, that I do my best work. My daughter and I are devoted to each other. When she was little and we were poor, my one great desire was to impress her.

'I wanted to do wonderful things to surprise her. Was it not for her that I became the woman that I am to-day? I succeeded. She had the greatest respect for me, just as I have for her! Our background of Alsatian discipline serves us both.

'I refuse to leave my office in the evening till I have disposed of all my work. Some people might think my life lacks gaiety. I should love, for instance, to go to Bagatelle to see the roses which, I am told, are a dream. I should also like to visit the Marie Antoinette exhibition at Versailles. Alas, if I went to one or to both of these places, hours would be wasted that I could never recapture. So from time to time I think about Marie Antoinette's jewels or the roses at Bagatelle—just as I sometimes listen to Beethoven on the gramophone while going on with my work.'

'Surely you have a few relaxations?' I asked. 'Most Alsatian women are excellent cooks.'

'Oh yes,' she answered, laughing, 'and what is more I am very greedy, though if I decide to dispense with a meal I can do so quite easily. As a girl I was brought up, of course, to be an excellent cook, and if ever you come to Orly, and let me know in time, I will make you a *choucroute au champagne* with all the ingredients from Mulhouse, which will simmer for four hours in a pot made specially for me by the village coppersmith. I will show you also the barbecue I have just built in my garden. This American custom, I understand, is catching on just as much in England as in France.

'My kitchen is almost a laboratory. Women have not yet fully understood that cleanliness should begin in the kitchen.

'I love to garden and I bring all my seeds from England. There is no greater pleasure than seeing what you have planted pushing its head up through the soil. I am up at six every morning, rain or shine. I pick great bunches of flowers and arrange them all over the house. I burn sweet-smelling herbs. Then I close each room and allow the house to slumber until, my work finished, I come back to it to enjoy serenely the last hours of the day.'

17

ANNIE, who looked after the show-cases at the
Plaza Athénée, and who had girl friends in all
the most famous dressmaking houses in Paris,
from Christian Dior to Balenciaga, called me as
I was hurrying out into the Avenue Montaigne
and cried:

'Did I hear you say that you wanted to meet Madeleine
de Rauch? I have a friend called Simone Prouverelle who
has just gone there from Fath's. Shall I ring her up and
ask her to introduce you?'

Simone Prouverelle, Annie told me, was quite her best
friend—a courageous young woman whose laughter hid a
terrible tragedy. Her little girl, who was exceptionally
pretty, had a squint. Simone was most distressed. Do
we not all want perfection for our children, especially for a
little girl? So, after much hesitation, Simone agreed to an
operation. She thought that the child, when she grew up
into a beautiful woman, would be grateful to her—but the
little girl died under the anaesthetic.

'Imagine how Simone blamed herself!' said Annie.
'After all, the operation had not been vital. It was merely
a question of vanity. And yet, Mme Henrey, what would
you have done? You would have done the same thing?
Of course! How could a pretty young mother not want
her little girl to be perfect? I implore you, however, do
not mention the matter to Simone. Like yourself she is
very sensitive. Even in this world of beautiful materials

and magnificent dresses round which we love to flutter there are tears in plenty!'

After telephoning to her friend, Annie explained that all I need do was walk down the Rue Jean Goujon. I loved this quiet street with its dressmaking establishments, its churches, and its sleepy, provincial-looking houses. I soon came upon a very splendid residence with an old-fashioned paved carriage entrance, and at the side, in very small letters, I read the words: MADELEINE DE RAUCH.

A staircase led me to the first floor, where a receptionist asked my name. When I told her that I was a friend of Annie's and that I had come to see Mme Simone Prouverelle, she gave me a friendly smile and hurried off to fetch her.

A few moments later a tall young woman of extreme beauty hurried towards me.

'I was expecting you!' she cried. 'Come into the *salon.*'

Immense windows looked out on the Place de l'Alma, and beyond one could see the Seine sparkling in the sunshine. I was surprised after coming up the rather sombre stairs to find so magnificent a room.

A woman, accompanied by her husband, was choosing dresses to wear at a fashionable resort in the south of France where they were going to spend an autumn holiday. The husband explained that they both liked to play baccarat and that his wife must therefore have dresses which would look nice when she was seated at the gaming tables, though of course, he quickly added, they must look equally effective when she enters the casino.

How pleasant for this woman to have a husband who liked to play baccarat and who was clearly so concerned about his wife's dresses. In the south of France casinos provide marvellous excuses for buying lovely clothes.

This husband was really full of attention for his wife.

'No, *ma chérie*,' he said quietly, with affection but with authority, 'that grey satin is dangerous. The green dress is more youthful and will make you look slimmer. Yes, believe me, the green one is much the prettier.'

The *vendeuse* agreed enthusiastically with monsieur. A man's opinion is very important. The men in Paris give their stamp of approval to restaurants and dressmaking houses. They are gourmets in food, and know what kind of dress suits a woman. When they go to dress shows it is not to watch the models but to crystallize fashion, if one may borrow an expression from Stendhal.

This particular husband was very pleasant to look at, middle-aged, with wide shoulders and an air of prosperity. I imagined him as owning an apartment in Paris, an American car, and a villa at Biarritz.

Several mannequins paraded in dresses. Simone Prouverelle came to sit beside me. She was delighted with her new situation. This house was distinctive amongst the great Paris fashion leaders for being entirely owned by Mme Madeleine de Rauch and her brilliant sisters. Sisterly love was the secret of its success.

A beautiful mannequin smiled at me each time she passed. I know nothing quite so delightful as being singled out by a mannequin whose smile suggests that she has chosen you out of all the other people in the room to smile at and be friendly with. She extends this visible sign of her affection by some secret accord. You smile back. The friendship is sealed. Every time she arrives in a new dress there is the pleasure of knowing that you are the elected friend.

'That is the sort of girl I should like to be!' I whispered to Simone. 'She is adorable to look at, just the right height, and has the most enchanting, tender smile.'

'Do not be too envious of her,' Simone answered. 'She

is the mother of two children both of whom are seriously ill, one with infantile paralysis. She is a very brave young woman, and I admire her tremendously.'

These words, coming from Simone, made me feel rather ashamed.

The show was over, and suddenly Madeleine de Rauch came into the room laughing. She had the laugh of a happy woman, she wore a light dress, and her blonde hair was extremely pretty. She came straight over to us and said:

'I must go out for a long walk. I have some important dresses to design for a wholesale house—very simple, not too many pleats, not too much material; but as they will go out under our name the work has to be perfect. That is modern! That is fun! I love it.'

Madeleine's sister, Germaine, joined us.

'We are four sisters,' said Germaine, 'all of us in the business—Madeleine, Suzanne, Yvonne, and myself. They call us the Whiteoaks of the Paris *couture*!'

'Or the Little Women!' said Madeleine, laughing.

'What a delightful idea!' I exclaimed. 'Have you always been together?'

'Germaine left us to marry M. Gounouilhou, who owned one of the most famous of our provincial newspapers, *La Petite Gironde* of Bordeaux,' said Madeleine, 'but at his death she very naturally came back.

'Father was an artists' colourman in the Rue des Petits Champs, near the Bank of France. We, the Bourgeois daughters, were open-air girls. I loved riding, Germaine was a champion skier, Yvonne won golf championships, and Suzanne was an excellent all-round sportswoman. As there was little difference between our ages, and as we were all considered good-looking, other girls noticed what we

wore and said they wished they could be dressed like the
Bourgeois girls.

'I married a Finn called M. de Rauch, who died penniless,
and so between the wars I decided to exploit my gift for
dress designing.

'My father found room for me in our house in the Rue
des Petits Champs, and I started by making sweaters which
women could pull on and off easily. Sweaters were warm
and pretty, and the vogue was in its early stages. My girl
friends came to me, and business expanded so quickly that
all my sisters gathered round me. The Bourgeois girls
became frantically busy. Suzanne even learned the art of
dyeing. Mother lent us her car to deliver the orders.'

Madeleine de Rauch explained how her early dresses
were relatively simple. Then suddenly she took to designing important evening dresses. These were soon to
bring her worldwide renown. Her laugh was that of a
very young woman, and she felt the need, she said, of a long
walk every day in the streets of Paris to find inspiration for
her work.

'Her steps are winged!' commented her sister Germaine.

She was born to colours, as indeed were all the Bourgeois
girls in the home of their father, the artists' colourman.
They opened their eyes on palettes, colour tubes, and the
splash of paint on canvas

A customer emerged from a fitting-room followed by an
essayeuse and a *vendeuse*. She was wearing a lace two-piece
suit of sugar almond pink, and slowly crossed and re-
crossed the *salon* so that she could assess how the elegance
of her *ensemble* stood up to the normal sway and movement
of her body. Intently she watched herself walking, and
we, who had stopped talking to follow every movement,
fell under the spell. This was not the sort of woman who
would allow *vendeuse* or *essayeuse* to flatter her. She knew
all about herself and was her own judge. She had reached

the age of experience when one tends to become long-
sighted. The mirrors in the fitting-room were doubtless
too close to her. After her third crossing of the big room,
which was bathed in sunshine, seemingly oblivious to
everybody and everything except herself and her suit, she
turned suddenly to Madeleine de Rauch and said:
'Truly, madame, you have made me a very beautiful
suit!'
The words fell with cold precision from her lips. One
sensed that customer and designer were women of similar
calibre who did not waste words. The customer returned
to the fitting-room, quickly followed by the *essayeuse* and
the *vendeuse*. A few minutes later she came out again in her
town clothes and crossed over to the door without so much
as turning her head in our direction.
I now learned what was perhaps the most human touch
in this story of family endeavour. The father of the
four Little Women was no more, but it was their mother
who bought this magnificent residence in which each
of her daughters except Suzanne had turned a floor into
a private apartment. Suzanne, who on every occasion
brought wise counsel, preferred to share a floor with their
mother.
This youthful mother of eighty-five thus had all her
daughters under her wing. Just now she and Suzanne
were in Biarritz.

An English mannequin was brought to us. She wanted
to know if Madeleine de Rauch would employ her. She
carried one of those box-like hand-bags which model girls
launched some time ago in London.
'Let her try on a dress!' said Madeleine de Rauch.
She came back a few moments later, her splendid body
tightly moulded in a black sheath dress in which she

paraded in front of us with snake-like movements, as if she were Salome trying to seduce Herod.

'We will let you know!' said Madeleine de Rauch.

The *couture* house was about to close down for the week-end, and Madeleine was anxious to set off for her walk. When the streets had provided her with the necessary inspiration, she would return to her beautiful apartment and allow future dresses to take shape under her crayons. Simone Prouverelle, who had left us, arrived wearing a superb white coat which, though loosely cut, had a few darts at the waist. The mannequin who smiled so sweetly at me while she was at work appeared wearing her own navy blue suit. She also was off for the week-end. An elderly *vendeuse*, whom I had noticed when the man who liked to play baccarat was helping his wife to choose a dress, came up to gossip.

'No,' she said, in answer to my query, 'I never go away for week-ends. I stay with my family. So you thought that our dresses were pretty, Mme Henrey? Yes, they are very youthful in design. I enjoy watching Jacqueline Joubert on TV because she is dressed by Mme de Rauch. What fascinates me is to see our lovely dresses reduced to the tiny dimensions of the screen, but Jacqueline Joubert is so full of life, that our dresses glitter and dance. I adore TV, Mme Henrey. I love everything that is new! Am I not fortunate to be in *couture*?'

18

HUBERT DE GIVENCHY was the most youthful of the great Paris dressmakers. Having become for the first time entirely his own master, dependent on nobody for financial support, this tall, studious young man of twenty-eight was fiercely determined to innovate.

'I have achieved freedom, and intend to take full advantage of it!' he cried with soulful intensity.

The house of Givenchy, some little distance from what was generally considered to be the heart of the dressmaking world, overlooked the carefully watered lawns and sandy walks of the beautiful Parc Monceau. Nurses with floating veils still embroidered and tacked hems while babies slept in prams and children played—a reminder of what Kensington Gardens must have looked like when J. M. Barrie wrote *Peter Pan*. The entire district breathed the staid air of the eighties. Even the street names were ultra-poetical, super-aesthetical. This one was Alfred de Vigny. I entered a courtyard where a man was washing down a car. The main residence was in front of me. To my right was a Gothic monstrosity with gargoyles, slated pepperbox turrets, and half-timbering over a red brick façade.

'This was once the home of M. Menier, the chocolate millionaire,' explained the man cleaning the car. 'These were the servants' quarters and harness-rooms. The stables were under the courtyard—the thick glass you are standing on allowed light to filter through. His carriage horses were led up and down a ramp.'

I crossed the courtyard into the main house where I was
joined by other women, smartly dressed, coming to see the
collection which took place every afternoon.   Oak wains-
coting and a massive oak staircase proved a sombre setting
for our light stockings and gay dresses.

Double doors with biblical figures carved massively on
them led into a large room where a great number of women
were conversing with their *vendeuses*.   I was immediately
noticed and questioned.

'Can I help you, madame?'

'I have an appointment with Hubert de Givenchy.'

My questioner looked suspicious but went over to her
desk to consult the appointment book, and I experienced
a momentary trepidation just as I do when I am asked to
hand up my passport to the stern Home Office official who
stands behind his desk at London Airport. Will he
suddenly find something wrong and send me to jail?

'I will tell M. de Givenchy that madame is here,' said
the woman, smiling.   She has seen from her list that I am
not an impostor.

There were lay figures dotted about the room, some with
white faces, others with black, and suspended from the
ceiling by wide blue ribbons was a chandelier with rams'
heads in tinsel.   The lay figures were dressed in waistless,
knee-length frocks, and for a moment I wondered if I was
back in the twenties.   Cardigans of pink and blue with
skirts to match were arranged over the backs of gilt chairs.
At the far end of the room immense windows opened out
on the beautiful lawns and rose beds of the Parc Monceau.
Children's voices filled the air.

A tall, supple figure suddenly cut a way through the
many women waiting to take their seats at the afternoon
show.

'Here is M. de Givenchy, madame.'

He had blue eyes, a tiny nose, and a tanned complexion.

A long tunic of almost Chinese design, closed by a single large button, showed the top of his tie and the folds of his soft collar. This tunic was beige in colour and made of such beautiful wool that one would have liked to stroke it as one strokes the binding of a valuable book.

He was attractively young, and the seriousness of his expression enhanced his youthfulness. His office was unpretentious and narrow, little more than a corridor, but through the windows one could see the top boughs of a tree that had its beginnings under the windows of the *salon*. I was nervous about this interview, for there are many questions that a woman finds it difficult to ask a man, and then again, a man's hobbies are different. He does not bring up children, knit, sew, or cook! If he often breaks successfully into the *couture* business, it is through the gift of drawing. Knowing how to draw is a man's only excuse for being a designer of women's clothes.

'My grandfather was a pupil of Jean-Baptiste Corot,' said Hubert de Givenchy. 'The gift of drawing was mine from birth. My father was closely connected with the tapestry manufactories of Gobelins and Beauvais.'

These de Givenchys originally came from the Pas-de-Calais, there being to this day a place called Givenchy-en-Gohelle, a coal-mining village seven miles from Arras, but Hubert de Givenchy's father married a girl from Beauvais, and it was in this cathedral city, where Joan of Arc was imprisoned and where the airship R 101 crashed in flames, that he was born on 28th February 1927.

Was he dull or clever at school?

'Not dull,' he answered guardedly, 'but drawing inevitably came first. I drew everything I saw, wherever I happened to be. And that I still do. At the end of the day I find that I have drawn on the same sheet of paper an idea for a dress, a picturesque corner of Paris, a hand-bag, a jewel, or a hat, and a group of children playing in the street. I draw from necessity as I breathe, and one idea leads happily on to another.'

He was destined for the law but his father died, and in his own words he was 'freed from the legal profession.' He was only thirteen when the Germans occupied France. Food became scarce and so his mother gathered up her two growing sons, of whom Hubert was the younger, and migrated to the richer province of Normandy, where she hoped to provide them with enough milk and butter to keep them in reasonable health. The food situation, under the maternal eye, became easier, but adequate schooling presented a problem which Hubert resolved by often playing truant to sketch the half-timbered barns and houses of this fiercely individualistic corner of France.

'At the age of seventeen, when the war came to an end,' he declared, 'drawing was the only thing I knew how to do!'

Circumstances had allowed him to pursue drawing to the exclusion of everything else, like the apprentices of great painters in medieval times.

A cousin gave him a letter of introduction to Jacques Fath—'that marvellous Jacques!' he called him—who hired him on the spot.

'I was mad with joy!' said de Givenchy. 'Only seventeen, and already working for one of the greatest houses in Paris!'

Genius, however, is restless. Even from this first moment of delirious joy, one sensed the *leit-motif* of his career to date—an irrepressible urge to achieve freedom! Freedom from convention was a phrase that constantly and almost savagely escaped from his lips. He was a Protestant, which in France implied all the Calvinistic rigour of a minority religion, and he said with an extraordinary look in his blue eyes:

'After a year and a half I went to Robert Piguet. I not

only admired the man as a great dressmaker, and his wonderful house, but he was also a Protestant—and after the years of German occupation I desperately needed a spell of Huguenot austerity!'

Were these not unexpected words from a young dress designer?

Even Piguet did not satisfy Givenchy's burning desire to penetrate the intricate technique of *haute couture*. From now on his moves were as carefully thought out as those of a chess player. He wanted to sample an organization such as Lucien Lelong's, an old-established house of wide renown.

'Without that sort of experience,' he said, 'one cannot successfully build up a house of one's own. I went to Lucien Lelong's at about the same time that Christian Dior was leaving it. We crossed like ships in the night.'

Then came the final lesson. He wanted to soar, to feel the full strength of his wings. René Gruau, the famous painter, sent him to Schiaparelli, who has been aptly described as the Picasso of the period.

'Oh, the enchantment of it!' cried Givenchy. 'I found myself surrounded by mountains of fabulous material. Mme Schiaparelli herself was dynamic and her clientèle was unique—women who dared to wear anything, and who wore it with extraordinary elegance. I have not, before or since, seen women with such magnificent jewels. My youthful enthusiasm burst into flame. I seeped myself in this atmosphere, appreciated what I saw, weighed each factor, worked without counting the hours.'

The *boutique* became his terrain.

I was about to ask him a question when the telephone rang and he asked my permission to answer it. His manners were perfect. I watched his long, narrow hand dart forward to take up the receiver, and almost at the same moment I became aware of a magnificent drawing by

René Gruau on the wall—the drawing of a splendidly proportioned hand, the fingers open to form a V through which an eye was visible. From this drawing my attention turned to a small satin-covered bust about six inches tall which stood on his desk. This miniature Venus, though without arms, legs, or head, was still obviously and deliciously feminine. The colour was rich garnet, and against the shoulder was pinned a tiny piece of lamé, so that my mind absurdly went back to Dumas's story of the three musketeers. Do you remember how they race to England to ask the Duke of Buckingham for the diamond which Anne of Austria gave him as a token of her love? Louis XIII, whose suspicions are aroused, tells her to wear it at a court ball. And in due course she wears it pinned on her shoulder like the piece of lamé on the shoulder of this satin bust.

Hubert de Givenchy, out of politeness to me, curtailed his conversation. When he had finished I said to him:

'Fashion writers have been telling us that nobody wants the small woman this autumn. Have you killed her?'

'I have killed nobody,' laughed Givenchy. 'That there are short women and tall women is one of nature's triumphs. Our business is to make pretty dresses for both kinds. Life would indeed be dull if all women were of uniform stature. The only things that I have killed in my present collection are those superimposed petticoats which created such a sensation in America. Though they were born in Paris, Americans were so quick to swamp the world with them that not everybody realized they were French.'

'What made you become a dress designer?' I asked him.

'My mother is a very beautiful woman,' he answered, 'and when as a beginner I left my pencil, while doodling, to its own devices, it was always her it started to draw! I would see her aquiline nose appearing on the paper!'

'What fun for a young man to design clothes for his mother!' I exclaimed.

Givenchy smiled.

'You are quite right. It would be,' he answered, 'but my mother is not fond of elaborate clothes. She is happiest in a jumper and a skirt. I have myself quite a passion for designing blouses. I give tremendous thought to them, because a skirt and a blouse are the clothes in which the greatest number of women, including the wealthiest, feel most at ease. After all, no woman wants to spend all day in a tailor-made or in a cocktail frock. So the right skirt and a pretty blouse or a sweater are indispensable.'

I recalled that quite a short time ago a Givenchy blouse with wide sleeves became the rage both in Europe and America. That must have been soon after he set up on his own.

'Yes,' answered Givenchy, 'I was twenty-five when, with the help of some relations, I rented two or three rooms in this very house. I began by making the clothes I loved and believed in—the skirt and the blouse. Joined together they became a dress. That was the birth of those "separates" whose fame became world wide. At that time I only had twenty-two workgirls, but I had the prettiest and most famous models in Paris, and I received the greatest encouragement from Carmel Snow in America.'

'The famous Bettina was one of your models, I think. Who was the other?'

'Ivy!' he answered. 'They wore my clothes so well, and people were so kind to me because I was the youngest *couturier* in Paris, the youngest in the world, that by the following year I was employing two hundred seamstresses. Most important of all, I was able to repay those relations who had come to my help at the beginning. The collection this autumn is my freedom collection. I need no longer listen to the counsel of others. When I created something

a little too new, too daring, I used to be told—which was
natural—that I ought to modify certain details in case the
dress did not sell.   I would be made to understand that if
I suddenly eliminated buttons or belts, for example, I might
antagonize people who specialize in these things.

'I have just launched a cunningly made elastic girdle.
The darts are so carefully thought out that it does not need
to be boned.   I like to see a woman walk and move in a
supple way.'

I suddenly asked him this question:

'If I arrived naked from another planet, M. Givenchy,
how would you dress me?   Will you not take up your
pencil and draw?'

He looked at me curiously.   I had taken him by surprise.
He said:

'Of course, it is not easy to create something entirely new
in a matter of seconds, but I know exactly what would
suit you.'

He took a sheet of paper and obediently, with his head
tilted on one side like a student—one could easily imagine
him being at a university—drew half of me full face.   I had
become half a woman!   He had given me a postilion's hat
and what at first sight might have appeared to be a three-
piece, but was in fact all one garment.   Well, I was fully
dressed!   He signed 'For Madeleine Henrey—Givenchy'
and handed me the drawing.   It was mine!   I owned my
first Givenchy dress!

I asked him if he smoked, for I had not yet seen him light
a cigarette, and his first gesture on meeting me had not been
to offer me one.   With many men it is more instinctive to
offer a woman a cigarette than to remember to ask her to be
seated.   No, he explained, he might feel the need of it if he
were nervous, but he was not nervous and so he did not
smoke.

I thought it time to explore this business of creating a

A madeleine Henry

Givenchy.

Paris dress. I was not entirely convinced that this young man merely doodled out the future line. How did he set about it? How did his mind work?

He was not sure whether he could give me this answer, but he would try to let me into his own way of thinking.

Had I noticed the lay models scattered about his *salon*? They were the same as those used so effectively in the windows of the big Paris store, the Magasin du Printemps.

'I find it essential,' he said, 'to have a certain number of the dresses I create continually in front of me. In this way two things happen. My eye becomes accustomed to the new line. Then when I have seen it for a certain length of time I get tired of it, and my immediate reaction is to start something quite different which will be to-morrow's line. That is how fashion is eternally reborn!

'Within this framework there are minor movements. When, for instance, I watch my models presenting a current collection I often think: "That is what I ought to have done!" "I should have lengthened this or shortened that!" So I go back to my drawing-board and try to improve. For this reason it occasionally happens that a new line will last, with only small modifications, for several seasons.

'Then again there is the rare moment of inspiration. I am in my office and I suddenly think about a woman I may have met during the last day or two. I might have noticed her at a cocktail party or at some private dinner. I think about her intensely. I try to recapture her every movement. Some men, when they see a pretty woman, mentally undress her. I do the contrary. My eye makes use of this living person to re-dress her as I think she ought to be dressed.

'I have been accused this autumn of creating extravagant hats, but it is in the hat that fantasy is born! When I made a drawing of you just now I started with the hat. Hats and shoes frame an elegant silhouette.

'On the whole I like the silhouette to be on the serious side. I have a positive horror of short, untidy hair. I like a woman to draw her hair back from her temples and to wear a bun. The bun has come back into fashion.

Nearly all the models in Paris now wear one. Long hair gives a woman dignity. No woman should ever believe that short, untidy hair hides wrinkles or a double chin!'

I ended by asking him two flippant questions.

'M. Givenchy, are you greedy?'

'Not in the least,' he answered, 'I hate sweets.'

'Then you are doubtless bad-tempered?'

'I would not have thought so,' he answered with a smile, 'but my mother keeps on saying to me: "My poor darling, how you work! How you fuss! Why don't you learn to keep still? Take a holiday!" "Yes, maman," I say to her, "you are quite right. I am extremely tired. I swing from enthusiasm to the wildest disappointments. A nasty criticism in a newspaper about some dress which has taken hours or days to create fills me with despair, but you must understand, maman, that if I had no collection to prepare, if there were no house of Givenchy, I should be perfectly miserable."'

He laughed a boyish laugh and added:

'As I was saying to you just now, Mme Henrey, I have chosen freedom—and if a man wants to keep his freedom, he must work his fingers to the bone!'

19

MANTES, the beautiful. That is what they called this little town, an hour's run from Paris, and almost on the borders of Normandy. All round were wheatfields, fine old houses, and forests in which the kings of France went hunting.

'Come out and spend the day with me,' Mme Jacques Fath had said to me on the telephone. 'I am resting after the strain of the collections, and happy to exchange the colours of a season's dresses for the russets and browns of autumn. Come! I will meet you at the station.'

There is no more intriguing personality in French *couture* than the beautiful young widow of the celebrated Jacques Fath who died so tragically a year ago. The world learned with surprise that the elegant Geneviève, whose beauty had graced the most brilliant parties in Paris, was determined to lead her husband's house to fresh triumphs—her own! Could she do it? people asked. One proof that she was able to was apparent during the historic week when President Eisenhower, Sir Anthony Eden, M. Edgar Faure, and Marshal Bulganin met in Switzerland to discuss the problem of world peace. The day that Lucie Faure, the French Premier's wife, gave her great ladies' lunch at the villa Prévorzier, five miles from Geneva, in honour of Clarissa Eden and Mamie Eisenhower, she chose a printed dress from the house of Geneviève Fath!

The Paris–Cherbourg express drew up, punctual to the minute, at Mantes. Geneviève Fath, in an adorable white wool two-piece, a warm creamy white, came forward to meet me. I was introduced to a Portuguese nobleman, the Duke of X, who took the wheel of the Cadillac to drive us to Mme Fath's château of Corbeville at St-Martin-des-Champs. The sun disappeared behind a cloud and there was a quick shower of rain, and as we passed a picturesque village all the ducks of the neighbourhood waddled and splashed in newly formed puddles, so delighted at this rain that they did not show the slightest fear when we sounded the horn. Now a tree-lined avenue, and ahead of us rose, as if placed there by some fairy for our delight, the prettiest little château. A narrow bridge over a grass-covered moat led directly to the entrance.

The influence of 'that marvellous Jacques,' as Hubert de Givenchy called Jacques Fath, was everywhere apparent in this beautiful place. I found it hard to believe that he would not suddenly come forward to greet me, the tall, elegant young man one of whose many hobbies was collecting paintings of dogs! Dogs in marble and stone, life-size or diminutive, decorated the terrace, while I discovered in every room paintings of greyhounds, sheep-dogs, boxers, and I knew not how many more breeds, by famous artists of all countries down the ages. These gave the château a curious throw-back to the sixteenth century of Henry III of France, who so loved dogs and lace. The rain had stopped and the sun was hot. The château has the pleasant even temperature of central heating in autumn. Mme Fath explained:

'A country house in which one is cold, or in which one must huddle in front of a fire, is not my idea of comfort. For a woman to feel at ease she must be able to wear what she likes. A cold house freezes both one's ideas and one's emotions.'

The Duke of X, who loved England, said:

'The English do not need to have warm country houses.

Their gardens are so full of colour that the flowers warm the house! In France the trees of our parks are distinguished but cold, like rows of solemn gentlemen in the diplomatic corps!'

Yes, perhaps he was right. We were all three seated in a pretty boudoir whose wide windows overlooked the main avenue of majestic trees, so alike in their width and height that I was quite surprised by such uniformity. Through these windows one could also see a well-tended lawn and, in the distance, a temple which Mme Fath told me was known as the Temple of the White Hind because Charles IX, who during his reign was so largely under the influence of his mother, Catherine of Medici, came upon a white hind there while he was out hunting. Did the lovely animal try to warn him against the massacre of the Protestants on St Bartholomew's Eve which was to haunt him for the rest of his life?

Geneviève Fath was a blonde with brown eyes and a light skin. Her rather long hair framed her face, giving it a gentle expression. She wore a narrow hair ribbon, the colour of gold, and she struck me as being extremely pretty.

There was a legend on both sides of the Atlantic that she started her career as one of her husband's mannequins.

'No!' she exclaimed. 'That is not true. Jacques was vexed when people repeated it. I was not tall enough. What I did was to serve as a model for hats. I have the right sort of a head. I was photographed in hats. I modelled them. I loved them—and still do!

'Between the wars we had some brilliant modistes in Paris, and *couture* houses had not yet started to show hats of their own. The *couturier* kept to his own business, the modiste to hers. Although I design hats as well as dresses I remain faithful to this custom in that I never show them together. I give my dress show at the same time as all the other great *couture* houses, and then present my hats later, for it is almost impossible for a buyer to take in at the same time a dress, a coat or a suit—*and* a hat!'

'There was a good deal of surprise, Mme Fath, when after your husband's death you suddenly decided to take over such an important house. People could not believe you had had enough experience. Nobody expected you to make such an amazing success of it. Had you ever designed a dress before?'

'Never, but every time Jacques gave me a dress he noticed that I started to alter it. I simply could not wear anything I had not adapted to my own needs. Jacques designed sumptuous dresses for me, ten at a time, but I remodelled every one. My friends accused me of being spoiled. They said I was frivolous and capricious, but no, unknown to myself I was passing through a severe apprenticeship. Male designers, however brilliant, are all the same. They draw a dress on paper and are satisfied to see it emerge into a fantastic, extraordinary, bizarre dress. A woman does not work that way at all. Her ideas do not come from pencil and paper but from the material which she crushes between her fingers during a fitting. Men know nothing about this. They see the dress of their imagination worn in ideal conditions by a mannequin, and think no more about it. A woman must live with her dress, like herself in it, and, what is more important, please others. Therein lies the difference in viewpoint between men and women designers.

'Madeleine Vionnet and Jeanne Lanvin stand out among their contemporaries as the great women designers who created dresses in which women themselves felt supremely happy. Paul Poiret and my husband—to take two examples—will be remembered for quite a different reason. They made dresses which it gave them pleasure, as men, to see women wearing. Of course, the man-designed dress is highly spectacular, and that is why it is often preferred by film-stars, famous actresses, or women prominent in society.

'Jacques proved a veritable maestro to a new generation of designers, and nearly all his pupils have done well and are known as splendid artists, whereas I am incapable of drawing a line. If I sometimes regret not knowing how to paint or to draw I console myself with the thought that Rembrandt might perhaps have shown thoroughly bad taste when choosing a dress for his wife, Saskia—and as for Renoir, though he painted adorable hats he could certainly not have made one.

'Women have such a diversity of interests. Mme Edgar Faure, for instance, though she is the Prime Minister's wife, and one of the busiest women in the land, adores coming to choose a dress. She is a pretty woman, but experience teaches one that prettiness has nothing to do with elegance. Many women whom at first sight I thought ugly became attractive and full of verve as soon as they try on a dress.'

Geneviève Fath's son, Philip, was twelve. Would he take after his father? She was not at all certain. He drew but that meant nothing yet. What surprised her was that she often saw him pause in front of a valuable piece of furniture, and then pass a finger lovingly across the wood. Would he become an art expert?

'When your husband gave receptions in this lovely castle were you impressed by the elegance of the women or were you inured to fine dresses?' I asked.

'Perhaps not inured,' she answered, 'but it was not until I went to Brazil with Jacques just before his death that I learned the meaning of surprise. Picture to yourself women of amazing beauty, with tiny feet, enormous eyes, and jet hair, the beauty of dark-haired women at its most perfect. I had seen some astonishingly beautiful Brazilian women in Paris, but here in France they are not surrounded

by their own people. They lack the exotic atmosphere,
the fierce sunshine, their native language. All this might
count for nothing were it not for the impression that love
lurks round every corner. How passionate those Brazilian
men are! What joy and torture they suffer in the name of
love! No wonder that in such circumstances women
blossom out like tropical flowers! They have American
air conditioning, our loveliest dresses, and the most captivating of Paris perfumes. Their jewels are unbelievable.
They love them, and their men love to see them wearing
them! Even the poorest little girls seem to share this love
for what is beautiful, and how could it be otherwise when
they are brought up in the contemplation of chasubles and
gold in churches?'

I noticed that Mme Fath was herself wearing a large
diamond solitaire of such purity that the blue-white stone
lit up her hand as she talked. When I remarked on it she
said:

'I am so glad you like it. I have a horror of costume
jewellery. At its best it is a lie. It destroys the beauty of
a great dress.'

The Duke of X put in:

'Amazing things can still happen in Europe. In my
own home in Portugal, for instance, there had stood in a
little-used room for as long as I can remember an enormous
chest of sacerdotal vestments which, as far as I knew, none
of my family had ever examined. I was curious to see
exactly what the chest contained, and so one day I opened
it and took out a great number of chasubles and dalmatics
woven in pure gold. After a time I came upon a curious
hat, a hat that must have been centuries old. The crown
was tall, and though it had lain under a great many heavy
vestments it had retained its original shape. I was most
intrigued. A hat quickly conjures up a picture. A dress
has to be filled out and worn but a hat is different. This

I

one immediately sprang to life. When I held it carefully
at arm's length in the dim light of the room, I had the
impression of seeing one of the medieval figures from a
painting by an old master in the Prado step out of its frame
and come towards me. My family, through the centuries,
has had its share of ecclesiastical and court dignitaries, just
as there had been churches and priories on our lands. I
was about to replace this curious hat when my attention
was drawn to a square ornament half hidden in the folds of
a moiré bow. I tore it off and slipped it into my pocket so
that I could have the pleasure of offering it to Mme Fath
in case she cared to wear it on a dress or a hat—or perhaps
was able to find inspiration from it.'

Geneviève Fath opened a drawer in a small writing-case
and placed in my hand a beautiful object which I took to be
enamel laid upon silver. One side portrayed St George
slaying the dragon. The saint's body was formed by a
large baroque pearl of unusual beauty, his features in
enamel showed clearly the strain of battle, the cheeks pale
with effort. The colours of this rare jewel were of the
brightest. Though a rosy mauve dominated the scene,
the grass was tender green and the sky of an exquisite blue.
Diamonds, pearls, topazes, and aquamarines studded the
surface. But I uttered a little cry of surprise when I saw
that the reverse was almost more beautiful—a riot of
coloured flowers, a daisy in the centre whose heart and
petals were formed by the pearl which, on the other side,
made the body of the saint.

She watched my delight and said:

'Having threaded it on a ribbon, I wore it as a pendant
at one of those fabulous parties that Señor Arturio Lopez,
the Chilean multi-millionaire, occasionally gives in his
fifty-room marble mansion at Neuilly. His ball-room is of
mother-of-pearl, he sleeps in a Louis XVI canopy bed, and
the rooms of his mansion are filled with rare silver and

furniture. He was bending over me, speaking polite trivialities, when his eyes suddenly rested on this jewel. '"My dear Geneviève," he exclaimed, "what have you here? Do not move, I implore you, lest you should drop this Renaissance masterpiece! Oh, please, allow me to buy it! I am a fervent collector of these rare marvels, and if I am to watch you waltzing round my ball-room with this treasure dangling from your neck I shall go mad with anxiety!"

'I am like Jacques. The only things he would sell were his dresses! He was so attached to this château, for instance, that returning to Paris from a trip to London he decided to entail it. English relatives had told him about this system, which set his mind dreaming. So neither I nor my son will ever be able to sell the home he so lovingly prepared for us. I shall be able to spend the rest of my life here. Nobody can drive me out. Jacques's mother, you see, was English. He admired the English way of life and the blonde beauty of English women.

'I was born in Brittany, and as I am a blonde I suppose it was the next best thing to being an English girl. I had a strong religious upbringing which does not prevent me from being, like all women, extremely superstitious! A picture that falls down fills me with dread that I shall hear of a death in the family. To dream of a cat means that I have an enemy. Dirty water foretells an illness. I am sensitive to the influence of the stars. I am a lioness!'

'So am I!'

'So you love dancing?'

'I adore it.'

'When I first knew Jacques, and he was courting me, we used to dance until daylight. He would then take a bath and go off to work while I went home to bed. It was amazing what inspiration Jacques found in these mad, glorious nights of dancing. The next day he never failed to produce a sensational dress—a dress that would travel round the world adding new lustre to his name!'

She placed the Renaissance jewel on a small table beside her and went on:

'In spite of his English mother, Jacques spoke English in the funniest way, but that merely added to his charm. What killed him at such an early age was the burning ardour which he put into everything he did. When he turned this château into a fairyland to enchant his guests from all over the world, he showed how successful he might have been in the theatre. I want my young son, Philip, to speak English without the slightest trace of accent. Before he was born I had so desperately longed for a girl. Now that I am alone I am glad to have a boy. He is at school at Les Roches, and during his holidays I generally take him to a small mill on the banks of the Loire which I have converted into a retreat of my own. Philip rides and fishes, and we can be together, just the two of us. The place is so deliciously small.

'I adore going to London. Vivien Leigh (Lady Olivier), who is a friend of mine, is surely one of the most perfectly beautiful women of our time. She can decide in a flash what will suit her and she is always so gay and amusing.'

Mme Fath asked me if I knew her.

'I was with my little boy at Shepperton studios,' I answered, 'when Vivien Leigh was making *Anna Karenina*, and I have a vivid recollection of the dresses your husband designed for her. She looked so naturally regal in her part that when I used to see her going home in the evening, a scarf tied over her hair, her beloved Siamese cat, whose eyes were the same colour as hers, tightly clutched in her arms, I could hardly believe it was the same person.'

I asked Mme Fath if she was a good cook. What did she give her little boy when mother and son were alone together in their mill on the Loire?

'Stews!' she answered with a ringing laugh. 'I make the most complicated stews which require infinite patience. Patience is one of my strong points. Perhaps that is because I am a lioness. I have the requisite patience, for instance, to lead a business undertaking successfully. Then, of course, being from Brittany, I am obstinate!

'One discovery I have made since taking over my husband's house is the ocean of difference that divides the women we dress from the models who present those dresses—not so much a difference in money as in concept. Married women are obviously influenced by the positions their husbands occupy, but there are other women, self-reliant women whose outstanding personalities must be studied and taken into account. There is an actress of the Comédie-Française who owns a magnificent diamond brooch, and who from time to time buys only a single dress which must be designed with no other end in view but to set off the brooch. When this superb actress goes out to supper she has more natural elegance than many women who have wardrobes full of fine dresses. Marie-Laure de Noailles, who leads Paris society and who is one of the last women to hold an intellectual *salon*, is quite extraordinary. At her home in the Place des États-Unis, so full of treasures, Jacques had the inspiration which led to the cut-glass bottle, in the form of a diamond, for the perfume Fath de Fath. Women such as Marie-Laure de Noailles influence Paris thought and fashion, and clearly they bring to a dress all their immense personality.

'Winter collections are the most exacting for a great *couturier*, because winter clothes must of necessity be more sumptuous than the summer ones whose lines they tentatively foreshadow. Winter fashions are expected to keep us warm as well as make us beautiful. Psychology often plays a part in the success of a collection. Have you ever noticed how often during a dinner-party, or at some reception, a woman will instinctively play with the pearls round her neck? This gave me the idea of adding to some of my dresses a flower or a tiny bow, so that those young women who did not yet have a necklace could innocently play with it.'

The sun, coming out strongly after another shower, turned the drawbridge into shimmering gold as I looked at it through Mme Jacques Fath's drawing-room windows. We had ranged over every subject and now she was telling me about a journey by car to the Midi. She was sitting next to the chauffeur and as they were crossing a bridge, the Pont de la Rose, near Gap, she heard him shout: 'Madame, we are going to have an accident!' The car leaped over the parapet and hurtled down a ravine.

'While we were spinning to what I expected to be death,' she said, 'a thousand thoughts crossed my mind. We were both injured, but as neither of us lost consciousness we saved ourselves from drowning by holding on to the doors of the car. We were rescued and I spent six months in hospital.

'Philip was then a baby, and as soon as I was well again I went to fetch him and his nurse back from the country. We were all four of us—he, the nurse, the chauffeur, and I —half way home when a lorry with a load of potatoes collided with us when trying to overtake us. This time I fainted. When I came to in hospital I found that though happily my little boy had escaped, the nurse was severely injured and the chauffeur was dead.

'I myself was in a very bad state—facial injuries, a broken thigh, and the same hand which had been injured in the first accident fractured a second time. I spent a year and a half recovering from these multiple injuries, and when at last I was sufficiently well to go out with my husband in the evening he made me, of course, the most beautiful dress.

A news photographer took a picture of me, and although I was still in great pain the picture, I must confess, made me look pretty. Alas, this was not altogether a blessing. The insurance company made use of this picture to prove that I was neither disfigured nor lame.'

Mme Fath laughed:

'I was undone by my love of finery!' she said gaily. 'But surely it was only to be expected that Jacques Fath's wife should wish to look pretty?'

The butler brought tea with little rounds of toasted French bread and red-currant jam made at Corbeville. Geneviève served tea but ate nothing herself, and afterwards took me to her bedroom, which was very prettily decorated in a green rust colour which made it fresh, restful to the eyes, and slightly old-fashioned. The furniture was Louis XVIII, and her bed charmingly placed in an alcove. Beside it there stood a photograph of Jacques, Philip, and herself—a happy picture. Her bathroom was quite adorable with bottles of Fath eau-de-Cologne and Fath perfume. A wide window overlooked the avenue with its tall trees.

We went down and inspected more of the ground-floor rooms, which opened into one another like the rooms at Hampton Court palace. This château was, in fact, a Hampton Court in miniature, with the same tall windows through which green lawns were visible.

Standing on the drawbridge was the chef wearing his tall white hat.

'Ah,' exclaimed Geneviève, 'there is the chef waiting for me! I have people to dinner this evening and so I shall go to market at Mantes. I like to buy the food myself, but I have just time to show you the swimming-pool.'

The swimming-pool was clear and blue, but its greatest charm lay in the fact that it was set amongst tiny eighteenth-century cottages all admirably restored and put to new uses. Thus one of them was for refreshments, another was a bar, and others, whose façades were covered with ivy, had been turned into dressing-rooms.

The Cadillac was waiting for us, but before we drove off the chef handed Mme Fath a shopping list.

Though it was nearly six, Mme Fath told me that the open-air market at Mantes would not yet be at its busiest. She was enthusiastic about this market, saying that the fish came straight from Trouville, the fruit from the Loire, and the butter and cream from surrounding farms. The road ran through cornfields which in harvest time must recall Millet's picture of the Angelus.

'I feel safe on this road,' said Mme Fath. 'I no longer enjoy long journeys by car and I am terrified every time we come to a bridge. On the other hand I love air travel, in which there are no mountain roads or precipices. Faster cars and trucks do not come up from behind with their screeching horns. I can relax in an aeroplane, and as I have no idea how the thing works I am happy to leave all the worry to the pilot, in whom, of necessity, I have complete confidence!'

She looked at me and added smiling:

'Men so quickly lose their tempers when driving a car. They want to show off or be spiteful to some other driver. The pilot has no such temptations.'

I smiled back at her in admiration. What an intense life she led! She was a mother, the owner of a château, head of one of the greatest *couture* houses in Paris. Her responsibilities were immense. She did not need to tell me that her chief desire was to be a good steward, to hand over these things, Jacques Fath's little empire, safely to her son when he came of age. Already she was busy planning a new collection.

More ducks waddled in rain puddles. We reached the station, which was full of workmen from Mantes factories.

Farewell medieval château, Hollywood film-star swimming-pool, rooms like Hampton Court palace! Farewell lovely Geneviève in your white wool suit! Beautiful was the diamond ring which hid the scar on your poor injured hand!

I squeezed into a compartment of the Paris train amongst tired men and factory girls whose cheap clothes smelt of sweat. My ear, always eager for human drama, attuned itself to a language which had nothing in common with that polished French I had just been listening to. Jokes were exchanged. I found myself laughing with the people in my compartment. Fath de Fath, the perfume I sampled in Geneviève's bathroom and with which my hand was covered, mingled with the pungent aroma of Maryland tobacco and the smell of machine-oil that stained the trousers of the workers. These were the tough ones, as they say in France. Once more I discovered that Dr Pangloss was right: 'All is for the best in this best of all possible worlds!'

20

ON a cold September morning I was standing at a fifth-floor window of a tall house in the Avenue Montaigne when M. Jean-Claude Donati came into the room and uttered these magic words:

'Mme Henrey, Christian Dior says that the place is yours. You may wander where you please, talk to whomsoever you wish, and come and go to your heart's desire!'

What a golden key to the world's most famous fashion house!

I stood quite still, feeling a little dazed. Where should I go? Upstairs or downstairs? What marvels, what unsuspected scenes awaited me? I tried to think. The autumn collections shown to press and buyers two months earlier had already become current fashion. The private customer had taken the place of the professional. The great house was presumably settling down to the routine activity of a Paris autumn season.

The original private residence in this lovely avenue, from which Christian Dior was to rise like a Napoleon to lead fashion throughout the world, was now almost dwarfed by the new building, in which, though it was so early in the morning, girls were stitching away as busily as Napoleon's legendary bees.

A few moments earlier, for instance, while on my way to this room, I came upon a dressmaker's dummy next to which a woman was working on some heavy black silk, and though I was immediately guilty of the sin of coveting a dress by Dior, I found myself wishing for something else first—to have the Venus-like proportions of this dressmaker's dummy, whose youthful breasts and rounded hips would have made any woman envious.

M. Donati's lieutenants were young women. One of them wore a loose-fitting jacket: she was expecting a baby. Another, very blonde, ceaselessly answered the telephone. The windows looked like brides with their white tulle curtains. M. Donati, having asked my permission to glance through his morning mail, paused from time to time to make some remark to me about his chief, whose portrait hung on the wall above us.

A man came into the office to tell us that he was just off to Singapore, and a moment later somebody else announced that he was flying to Colombia. The house of Dior continued to extend its far-flung but innocent empire. A secretary was stamping a mountain of envelopes addressed to the ends of the earth all bearing those romantic initials 'C. D.,' which hitherto I had mainly associated with the motor-cars of ambassadors and other members of the Corps Diplomatique. Here they stood for the paradise that every woman longed to enter and which, even to those of us who would never own a Dior dress, evoked a pair of stockings or a drop of Miss Dior perfume.

'M. Dior, who wants to meet you later in the week when you have had an opportunity to look round,' said M. Donati, opening a letter with a foreign stamp, 'adores the country. His hobby is planting trees. Sport he considers barbarous. Music, the pleasures of the countryside, and dress designing dominate his every thought. Pardon me! I must answer this telephone. . . .'

'M. Dior,' he continued, putting down the receiver, 'always chooses his own mannequins, and he does not choose them merely for their beauty. Oh no! They must have something—what shall I call it?—something that long before the Anglo-Saxons coined the term sex-appeal we, in France, called chic. Our girls never smile. Each one of them has her own personality. M. Dior discovers it in them and then shows them how they must develop and retain it, so that in no circumstances will they ever merit that odious name of "clothes-horse."'

M. Donati's telephones all rung at once. Excitement was tense. I went down into the airy rooms where already, in preparation for the afternoon show, gilt chairs were arranged in rows. Here, each day, one of the greatest shows on earth took place. No stage performance was so eagerly sought after. None was so difficult of entry. What happened in these rooms would later be described in the four corners of the world. In a few hours, smiling but implacable guardians would stand at the top of these stairs to scrutinize those who came to witness these enthralling variations on a theme of elegance.

Should I watch the show again? As I was so privileged I would go backstage and see it from the models' changing-room! This exciting prospect filled me with delight.

I ran down to the *boutique* where a young blonde was in charge of a sort of Fountain of Trevi which, without the need of a coin being thrown into it, magically sprayed one with Dior perfume. Perhaps, like the girls in the film, I should have made a wish! Every time I passed the fountain I was sprayed with more Miss Dior! I could hardly tear myself away from this captivating amusement.

Moved by an inexplicable impulse, I ran right to the top of this fairy palace. Here I was on the seventh floor! The windows, faithful to the loveliest form of French architecture, were attic windows, but the walls were painted the softest green and the floors were the colour of bright sunshine.

I discovered a door on which was written the word REPOS. This was obviously a rest-room. I pushed it gently open and found the sort of couch one sees in the more expensive beauty parlours, and as I was out of breath I lay down on it; but my presence had been noticed, for another door opened for just long enough to bring me the sound of feminine laughter. Standing over me now was the house doctor!

She was an adorable woman in the early thirties who, by the soft expression of her eyes and by the mobility and gaiety of her features, quite captivated me.

'I am Dr Suzanne Py!' she said.

She wore a becoming white garment that had a military collar and a pocket over the left breast bearing the magic initials 'C. D.' At first I said to myself: 'She looks more like a beauty expert than a doctor!' But I soon changed my mind. Dr Suzanne Py was a serious young woman.

She sat at a small modern desk, a bowl of zinnias at her elbow, put on spectacles, and consulted some files.

'I am kept busy all day with minor accidents, illness, or fainting fits,' she explained. 'Just now, for instance, I was with a woman whom we call in the dressmaking world a matching girl, because her business is to cross and recross Paris in every direction to match a button, a feather, an odd length of material, or a piece of braiding, embroidery, or lace. She knows every firm that specializes in these things, and her life is spent hurrying from street to street. She was knocked down by a car the other day, and as her injuries did not appear at all serious, the insurance company acting on behalf of the motorist was anxious to dispose of the case as quickly and as cheaply as possible; but it is my business to protect her in case complications arise.

'I qualified at the age of twenty-six. My father and my grandfather were doctors. When, as a girl, I announced my intention to take up medicine my parents exclaimed: "My little Suzanne, you don't really want to be a doctor. You are merely influenced by seeing so many doctors in

the family. Doctoring is no profession for a woman!"
They were wrong. I knew exactly what I wanted, and so
here I am, one more young woman working for Christian
Dior! I love doctoring and I adore fashions! I have not
had time yet to see the winter collection, but I am longing
to do so, because I follow the progress of every new show
from its earliest beginnings to its triumphal revelation to
the world. I know what the rest of the world knows
nothing about—the anxiety, the keyed-up nerves, the
intense fatigue, the private tragedies, the bravery of the
girls who stitch with fairy fingers those magnificent dresses
that fire the imagination of women everywhere.

'There was a young woman, for instance, who instead of
developing as she should have done seemed to do the
contrary. She was what we call *une deuxième main* who
adored her profession of seamstress, but her mother died
and her father married again. This new marriage resulted
in a large family which she was made to look after. She
was the first to get up in the morning. She made breakfast, looked after the babies, went to market, and prepared
the vegetables before she came to work. She was so afraid
of being beaten that she never complained, and it took me a
long time to discover her unhappy secret. I went to see
her father and now I have sent her to one of our rest homes,
where she is pitifully surprised to discover so much
kindness.

'We vaccinated nine hundred employees against small-
pox the other day, and as they are nearly all women we did
it on the thigh so as not to leave a disfiguring scar on their
shoulders. In a few cases the vaccination caused a slight
inflammation. The girls all persuaded one another that
they were starting some appalling illness they had been
reading about in their favourite women's magazine!
Looking as fresh as daisies, they hurried up to me, quite
certain they had an illness with an unpronounceable name!

'Sometimes a girl will prick herself rather badly with a needle—that generally produces three patients, the one who has pricked herself and two companions who faint in sympathy! Then there is the girl who holds a hot iron near her cheek to test its heat, and turns round too quickly to talk to another girl. There are those whose shoes pinch and so they leave them under their chair, walk across the room in their stockinged feet, and drive a stray pin into their soles! But most important of all are the young mothers! They leave six weeks before the baby is due and do not come back until five weeks after it is born. M. Dior presents a complete layette in each case, with the result that every little boy and every little girl starts out in life dressed from head to foot by Christian Dior! So if the little boy does not become a great dress designer, and if the little girl does not turn into a lovely model, it is not for want of inspiration!'

21

ITOOK leave of pretty Dr Suzanne Py, and tried to
find my way back to the stairs, but, like Bluebeard's
wife left to wander freely about the house, I opened a
little door and came upon a most unexpected sight—
the two men and the young woman who make
Christian Dior's Cinderella-like shoes!

I told them I had lost my way. Manuel Mantilla, as he
looked up from his bench, revealed severe but regular
features. He was a Spaniard, and in front of him were
tiny wooden forms whose steep curves puzzled me until I
realized that they would compensate for high heels. How
dainty they were! How free from bunions and corns!
Manuel Mantilla, I reflected, must have been making shoes
for a princess who was accustomed to walking on rose
petals!

Born in 1907, son of a famous shoemaker, he spent his
childhood travelling from one European capital to another
because of the varying fortunes of his father's trade.
Then one day he became a shoemaker himself, married a
French girl, and settled in Paris.

'Oh no, madame!' he cried. 'It is not easy to create
anything new in ladies' shoes. Bear in mind the tiny
surface we work on, and the centuries and centuries since
cunning shoemakers first plied their trade! Occasionally
one has an idea. That is heaven, but it is always nice to be
working with leather that is soft and beautiful. When I
go out into the street I never pay attention to the passing
scene. No, madame, my eyes sweep the pavement. I

look at feet! Some people say that I look sad when I walk along the street, but they are wrong. I enjoy myself prodigiously.

'I have a son but he will not be a shoemaker. Times are changing, you see. I love my trade so much that the hours slip by in pure delight, but to-day a young man learns shoemaking in a technical school, and that is not at all the same thing. Master shoemakers of old were mean with money but generous with good advice. We worked till late every night. In short, madame, shoemaking was a labour of love as it still is in parts of Italy. The Italians are the cleverest. Rumanians are good and Spaniards, my compatriots, come next. The foot, madame, is a southern speciality.'

Manuel Mantilla's companion-aide, Marguerite Gugli-otta, who was of Italian parentage, sewed tiny strips of leather with deft fingers. Roger Vivier, a Parisian, in shirt-sleeves and vivid red braces, declared that when he was a boy, instead of drawing little men with tall hats and strange faces he drew shoes, always shoes, and as they buttoned up at the sides in those days he pretended the buttons were eyes.

'Drawing shoes was an obsession, madame. Friends who came to visit my parents owned a little shoe factory. Instead of laughing at me they took one of my drawings away and had the shoes made up. Imagine how proud I was!

'I plunged into shoemaking. I tramped round Paris, searching for ideas, and one day in 1937, while looking at a stall in a second-hand market, I came across a very old and tiny Chinese slipper which I bought for a few shillings, but with which I was so delighted and intrigued that I was trembling all over. I tucked it safely into my pocket, where it weighed no more than a feather, but it occupied my every thought.

K

'A close study of these Chinese slippers resulted in my invention of the platform shoe which set my heart pounding with joy when the first one was put into my hands; but my happiness quickly turned to tears because when I sent it to New York I was told that it was not nearly dainty enough for American women to wear. Broken-hearted, I telephoned Mme Schiaparelli, who was so delighted with it that she featured it in her next dress show. The platform shoe was born, and all feminine Paris walked on it during those terrible years of the German occupation when soles could only be made of wood or cork.

'I was not in Paris to witness my tardy success. I was in New York during the war, where, as a change from women's shoes, I opened a shop for women's hats. The extremities have always exercised a fascination for me. Mme Schiaparelli, the Duchess of Windsor, and Marlene Dietrich were amongst my customers. After the war, tired of hats, I returned to my first love and started to make shoes again.

'Colour plays an important role in shoemaking. The fashion for pastel-coloured shoes which proved so popular this summer was launched by me, but it took me two years to popularize those delicate pinks and blues, and now I can no longer stand the sight of them.

'Women's feet are unquestionably growing larger. Ballerina shoes, sports shoes, and too much walking are responsible for this. Those sandals, revived from ancient Greece and Rome, were never designed for Anglo-Saxon feet. Spanish women retain a traditional smallness, but their feet are plump. English women have a long and narrow foot, but curiously enough all the female members of the Royal Family—the Queen, Princess Margaret, and the Queen Mother—have unusually small feet such as men on the Continent admire.

'When you go down into the shop, madame, ask Brodsky,

a Russian from Kiev who presides over it, to show you my famous shoe made of white mink! They have been reproduced in newspapers and magazines all over the world.'

When later my wanderings brought me to this part of the Christian Dior wonderland, my eyes turned to a young woman who was in earnest conversation with a young and pretty employee.

'My shoes are perfect,' said the customer. 'I am delighted with them, but I am not happy about the gloves. Do go and buy me another pair—a black pair with nice long fingers. Choose them for me, my dear.'

'You will have to give me some money,' answered the employee.

The elegant customer opened her bag and handed the young employee her wallet. She peeled off a glove and a beautiful diamond solitaire threw out rays of fire from her finger.

When the customer and I were momentarily alone, we smiled at each other and I said to her:

'You appear to be on very friendly terms with that pretty employee.'

'Oh yes,' answered the customer. 'She is my daughter.'

'You certainly do not look old enough to be her mother!' I exclaimed. 'Are you in the textile business yourself?'

'Oh no,' she laughed gaily. 'Quite the opposite. I am Mme Hennessy!'

We went into raptures over the new high heels that were scarcely thicker than a needle. Though Mme Hennessy was one of the French branch of the 'Three Star' family and the wife of a millionaire, we were just for the moment two excited women gasping a little in surprise at these amazing shoes. We discovered a model in beaver with topaz heels, and then there were other heels capped with

interchangeable cut-glass ends.   Oh, shades of Cinderella!
How could anybody pretend that the days of fairy-tales
were over.

Every new door I gently pushed open brought me some
fresh cause for wonder.   Here was a young man called
Jean-Marie Roucher with a secretary.
'The waste-paper-basket did it!' he exclaimed.   'That
stupid waste-paper-basket!   My secretary tries out new
Dior nylons.   She has been wearing these for forty-five
consecutive days, washing them every night, and they
might have lasted for ever had it not been for that waste-
paper-basket.   Look!   She has a ladder!'
'Alas, I know the feeling,' I murmured sympathetically.
'M. Dior would not have designed nylons,' said the
young man, 'if elegant women had been more careful of
their hose.   He was pained to see so many of his dresses
worn with wrong stockings.'
'What are right stockings?' I inquired.
'Colours that harmonize with M. Dior's collections, and
no black seams or exaggerated heels.'
The young man started to tell me that M. Dior had hit on
a very pretty way to show his nylons.   They would be put
in picture frames all along the wall as if they were paintings
in an art-gallery.
'Picture frames?' I queried.
My thoughts flew back to the years between the wars.
A young man whom many regarded as a promising artist
himself had organized the first exhibition of Christian
Bérard's paintings at a picture-gallery in the Rue Camba-
cérès in Paris—a shy young man who could be seen looking
up at the pictures in the picture frames wondering about
his own future.
That young man was none other than Christian Dior!

22

I SCARCELY heard M. Christian Dior, so silently did he slip into his office. I was standing in the middle of the room, the colour scheme of which was a mixture of ebony and honey, and I was vexed, having just discovered the loss of a button from the jacket of my tailor-made. It was not that I had any hopes of impressing M. Dior with the elegance of my person, but I knew him to be a man with an eye for detail.

He offered me a hand as cool and gentle as that of a cardinal. I could easily have pictured him dressed in the scarlet robes of Cardinal Wolsey. His complexion had a slight tan, his features an air of repose as if he were too strong-minded to allow anything to worry him, though heaven knows his worries and preoccupations must have been numberless. His autumn collection was only just making its appearance in public, but already his mind was preoccupied with something new for the spring.

Behind him, as he sat at his desk, was a photograph of the Countess of Paris, with her daughters, on another wall a photograph of Princess Margaret.

He was born at Granville, pretty little Norman seaside resort on that peninsula that culminates in Cherbourg, and he told me that he hoped to go there at the end of the week to do some fishing, for which a spell of cloudy weather would be welcome.

Already in imagination he was back in the place where he was born, for he began to talk about a strange adventure that happened to him when he was twelve.

'There was a *kermesse*, or fair, at Granville that particular summer,' said Christian Dior, 'and the boy does not live who does not take a delight in such things.   I went into a booth where a fortune-teller was reading the future in a pack of cards.   I remember her name to this day.   She was called Mme Ducros.   She foretold some curious and rather terrifying things, that I would be ill and poor, but that I would eventually achieve astonishing success thanks entirely to women!'

M. Dior's parents, if he told them this, must have been rather taken aback, for at that time he was destined for the diplomatic service.

'I steadfastly believed in this prediction,' Christian Dior continued, 'and before long the bad part of it came true, for which reason I believed in it even more because I said to myself: "If the first part has happened, the second part is sure to happen also."   So in my darkest moments I was full of hope.   I sensed vaguely that women would bring me luck.

'So I am bound to admit that even to-day I am superstitious, and every time I show a new collection I manage to pin a small posy of lilies of the valley on a dress or a coat. Lilies of the valley bring me luck both winter and summer.'

'Are you superstitious about colours?'

'No, except for violet.   I never show any dress of the colour of that tender and modest flower in a collection.   I am fond of green.   I adore red.   I fancy one is apt to adjust one's personality to different colours.   For no particular reason, for example, I am doing up my new home in Paris in red and green, whereas blue and yellow are the dominant colours of my home in the Midi.'

Christian Dior!   This magician had a simplicity and a modesty which formed an endearing mantle to his genius.

I frequently caught a glimpse of him as I explored this wonderland of which he had given me the key. Always he moved across a room, up or down a staircase with silent steps, bashfully, as if it hurt him to be recognized. His personality was everywhere. When he gave an order it was in a low voice. There was never an argument. After his instructions had been carried out the full measure of his wisdom became clear—and not only his wisdom but that youthfulness of conception, renewed so frequently, which had allowed him to remain for so long the most discussed figure in his profession.

In Paris the mannequins' changing-room is known as *la cabine des mannequins,* but the Dior girls called it the swimming-pool.

The room did, in fact, strangely evoke an indoor swimming-pool, rectangular in shape, large enough to allow ten of the prettiest girls in the world, with their dressers, to move about comfortably under the supervision of Mme de Turkheim, the 'Baroness,' who was *chef de cabine*—an adorable mother hen who sent her daughters out to the ball, one after another, a ball that started without music at three every afternoon.

Round the room was a gallery lined with deep wardrobes in which were kept the dresses, suits, coats, and hats to be worn during the three-hour show, and along the balcony flitted Corinne, playing a perpetual Juliet to the dressers below as they shouted for the garments they needed:

'Send down the Mystery of New York!'

'Hurry up with that Samarkande!'

Whereupon the dress, freshly ironed, sometimes even repaired if there had been an accident, was lowered down on its hanger into the dresser's arms below, while another dress, which some model had just taken off, was fixed by its hanger to the hook of a pole and handed up to Corinne to put away.

Each girl had a section of the wardrobe wearing her name, and the names of the fifteen or twenty dresses which she would be wearing during the show, written clearly above it. Thus I read:

VICTOIRE	wearing Pomme de Pin and so on
LUCKY	wearing Mystery of New York and so on
ODILE	wearing Orient Express and so on
RENÉE	wearing Aventure and so on

Alla, the wonderful Alla, known amongst her colleagues as The Pearl of the Orient, was not present. She had carried on for the first month of the Y-line with a high fever, and was now in bed trying to recover. How could she possibly have missed the first night and subsequent vital showings, considering that she measured only $18\frac{3}{4}$ inches round the waist, so that it was almost impossible to find a girl to take her place. Daughter of a Russian father and a Chinese mother, she was born at Kharbin. She never intended to be a model. One day she arrived with a friend and rather nervously asked to see Christian Dior, who immediately engaged her.

Corinne did her ironing on a wide board which was as firm as a rock. Her irons, which had none of those terrible flexes, were heated in a small electric oven kept constantly at the right temperature, and she went backwards and forwards to her oven like the ironing women of a generation ago, all of which goes to prove that the old-fashioned often becomes the ultra-fashionable!

I watched her iron, unshackled by flex, speeding up and down a long dress, and for the first time I realized the unsuspected workmanship revealed by a Dior dress turned inside out on an ironing-board so that every seam, pleat, dart, and flair was visible.

Corinne knows every dress by its name. They are as human to her as are the models who wear them. To watch Corinne ironing is—if you are a woman—to have a wonderful lesson. While the dress is still warm from the iron she slips it on a hanger, puts it back in the wardrobe, then deftly starts work on another.

Below, on the floor of the 'cabin,' the models came and went, undressing and dressing with a precision that filled me with admiration.

Claire—who was the Countess of Billy—stepped into a dress while, with movements almost too fast to follow, she put on a hat, fastened a pair of earrings, and slipped on elbow-length gloves. When both Claire's legs were in the dress, the dresser pulled up the long fastener while Claire held her breath to allow it more easily to imprison her tightly in the sheath. The zip reached the top. Claire, like a graceful cat, stretched into position under the appraising eye of Mme de Turkheim. A few seconds later I heard the name of her dress being shouted out in the *salon* to the assembled audience, many of whom had come thousands of miles just to see this collection. The audience were as excited as at a theatre or opera, for was this not one of the greatest shows on earth?

Corinne put down her iron to answer the telephone.

'No, monsieur,' she said firmly. 'Mademoiselle CANNOT come to talk to you. We are in the middle of a collection.'

She replaced the receiver and took up her iron again, but all the models, dressing or undressing in the 'swimming-pool' below, called out:

'Corinne, who was it? A husband, a cousin, a grandfather, or a boy-friend?'

'I don't know,' answered Corinne. 'It was just a man! But don't worry. He is sure to ring again!'

A dresser called up to say that her model would be ready in a moment for her Persian evening dress. Corinne went to the wardrobe and beckoned to me as she brought it out: 'See this marvel with its pure Persian design embroidered with thousands of coloured pearls!' she exclaimed. 'Take it in your hands and feel the weight of it!'

There were flashes of yellow and turquoise as I took it from her. The design sparkled against a background of heavy ivory satin, and, as Corinne warned me, it was heavy, so heavy that one felt it would stand up by itself.

'Oh!' I whispered, afraid to raise my voice in the presence of such splendour. 'I would never dare to wear it!'

Corinne smiled up at me. What a sweet girl she was in her little black dress as she ran about her gallery, stood in front of her ironing-board, fetched a dress worth a fortune or put one away! How gay she was as she suddenly heard a girl down in the 'swimming-pool' say something funny! Then swift came the repartee, as brilliantly clever as you would expect to hear from any actress on a boulevard stage! I loved her already as, with her permission, I held this dress in front of me. See! I was no longer in a home-made jumper and skirt. I was a princess from the land of the Arabian Nights! Did not my blonde head emerge from above a dress worth as much as a house? I was almost beautiful! Or was I dreaming? If, after I am dead, somebody opens my heart, will they find written in letters of yellow and turquoise: 'She once thought herself pretty from behind the loveliest of all lovely evening dresses by Christian Dior!'

The models were not allowed to make the slightest impromptu variation in their *ensemble*. Occasionally one of them would have liked to go out into the *salon* wearing another girl's hat. Mme de Turkheim quickly prevented her from doing so. Looking down from the balcony I saw Francine for fun trying on a tiny red hat, no larger than is required to hide a chignon, belonging to another girl. She probably wanted to see if this red hat would suit the red dress she was wearing. She looked at herself in the mirror and tossed it aside as if it had burned her. The truth is, I reflected, that however unwelcome it might sound to us, men know better what suits us than we do ourselves. We approach the lovely things of fashion as though entering a garden to pick flowers. We want to wear every dress within sight, try on every hat, just as we like to pick all the prettiest flowers in the garden for our posy. Men realize that certain types of dress, certain types of hat, suit certain types of women.

Lia was Rumanian, and we took to each other at first sight.

She had magnificent chestnut eyes, the whites of which were very white—oriental eyes, as were the fashion that winter—with auburn hair resembling the colour of the leaves of the chestnut-tree in autumn. I had gone down to talk to her and was soon enchanted by the way she rolled her r's, for I cannot resist the Slav accent. She stood facing a group of us in her white girdle and nylons. Three rose-buds with a piece of green ribbon for a leaf gave a minute splash of colour on the left hip of her white girdle.

'Why the bouquet?' we all asked.

'Because,' she answered, putting on her long gloves for the next appearance in the *salon*, 'I have been a good girl and a cabinet minister has just decorated me!'

She was behind the Iron Curtain till 1950, engaged in advanced studies at the university. Her lovely eyes enveloped me as she commented:

'I am a political refugee!'

I was desperately eager to hear her story. She told me that on the ship which brought her from Constanza to Marseilles a steward said to her: 'You ought to be a model!'

So she followed his advice. 'And now,' she added with delight, 'here I am amongst all these pretty things!'

Lia, wearing only her white girdle, stockings, and black gloves, had to be dressed, so I returned to Corinne. A mannequin in a white dust-coat sat reading a book near the ironing-board.

'The newest girl has to sit beside me on the balcony,' explained Corinne, 'so that naturally I soon become very attracted to her. The day Odile left me to go down into the 'swimming-pool,' for instance, I cried my eyes out. This is Valéry.'

I suddenly remembered seeing this girl when she arrived. She intrigued me as I watched her frantically searching in her hand-bag for a key with which she opened a little desk. From this desk she extricated a hand mirror in which she proceeded to make up her eyes, pushing her face right up against the glass. I saw her eyes gradually become larger and more expressive under the kohl. Very cunningly she applied with a pencil those little lines that give one what are known as hind's eyes. She then made up her lips.

I reminded her of this, and she explained:

'I am terribly short-sighted, but once I get to know a place I can manage without my glasses. One day M. Dior watched me putting on my hat. Afterwards he said to me: "I don't think you have put your hat on straight, and yet you were in front of a mirror. Are you short-sighted?" "Yes, M. Dior." "Well, Odile is short-sighted also and she is one of my best mannequins. That often happens with short-sighted girls. They have that rather vague look which enhances their beauty."'

Corinne had gone to the wardrobe to fetch another magnificent evening dress. I asked Valéry what she wore in the show.

'A very simple black worsted,' she answered. 'It sells like hot cakes.'

An angry voice came up from below. It was that of Mme de Turkheim.

'Why has this zip fastener not been replaced?'

'But, madame, I assure you that it has.'

'Then it must be a *vendeuse* who tried this dress on a customer and broke the zip!' said Mme de Turkheim. 'Customers always insist on trying to get into dresses made for models. The saleswomen flatter them and then accidents happen. Not surprising when you remember that one model often cannot get into a dress made for another girl!'

'My stocking has laddered!' cried Valéry.

'Very well,' said Corinne. 'I will see that you are given another pair. You have been a good girl.'

Corinne turned to me and explained:

'At the start of each collection the girls are given a Dior girdle, a brassière, and some stockings. All the girdles and the brassières are white.'

'When I have been here for six months,' said Valéry, 'I shall be allowed to choose for myself one of the models I wear in the show. In some *couture* houses the girls are allowed to borrow clothes to wear in the evening, but that is forbidden here.'

Odile, beautiful brunette, a daughter of the hot Midi, returned. During the show she wore her hair in a chignon. Now she was letting it down. Lia hurried in, and taking off a tiny feathered hat placed it on the head of a dresser who was removing another girl's foundation garment. Lucky, a lovely girl from Brittany, entered like a gust of wind to answer the telephone. She wore her chignon in a point high on her head. Claire, the beautiful Parisian girl, returned in her superb wedding gown. The show was over. I had watched the greatest show on earth from the wings.

23

THOSE warm September days were full of charm. In shop windows the first winter coats were being displayed, but in the street could still be seen cotton dresses and those pastel-coloured shoes that Roger Vivier had made fashionable and of which he was already tired. Next year we were likely to see even more of them, because women who did not dare buy them when they were a novelty might well scramble for them as soon as the novelty wore off. There are, happily for the shops and stores, three stages in every new fashion. Truly elegant women adopt it the first year, those who are more prudent the second year, and the masses the third year when it is on the verge of disappearing.

I spent the morning trying on hats at Christian Dior's, keenly alert to everything that was going on about me. The woman in charge of the *salon* exclaimed to a neighbour:

'No, madame, we will make you a hat that fits your head perfectly. These are worn by the models for a few short moments as they pass through the rooms every afternoon showing off the clothes, but you, madame, need to have a hat in which you cannot merely walk, but talk and laugh.'

A tiny red and black feather hat, as light and colourful as an exotic bird, peeped out of the half-open drawer of what was virtually a shorthand-typist's desk. This little hat tossed into semi-obscurity was certainly not for sale, but by some remarkable coincidence every woman in the *salon* had caught sight of it and was dying to try it on.

'No!' cried the saleswoman. 'This hat is reserved for a

customer whom I am expecting at any moment. Imagine
how vexed she would be if she walked into the room and
found her hat on another woman's head! Please do not be
angry. We can always make you one like it.'

She turned to me and whispered confidentially:

'What is it that makes them all want the one hat they
cannot have! Every time we hide a model some customer
catches sight of it, and it at once becomes magnetically
attractive.'

In the centre of the room was a round table covered with
a plush rug the borders of which fell to the ground. Scattered pell-mell on this table were all the hats worn by the
models during the collection—the lovely hat, for instance,
which Claire wore so becomingly and which Corinne
wickedly nicknamed 'a flowerpot turned upside-down,' but
which when Claire, still in girdle and brassière, put it on
made Corinne exclaim: 'That hat is madly clever. One
laughs at it and cries out in admiration in the same breath!'
Here also was the tiny red hat, no larger than was required
to hide a chignon, that I saw Francine trying on to discover
if it would suit the red dress she was wearing. As I took
these hats up to examine them I was charmed by their
cunning workmanship. They were simple, elegant, and
ladylike.

Though it was already one o'clock, the various *salons*
showed no lessening in activity. Wealthy women from
foreign lands passed slowly from the millinery to the
boutique, pausing to examine magnificent furs.

Suddenly there was a murmur of excitement. A woman
who between the wars wrote a sensational page of contemporary history ran lightly up the stairs. She was
hatless and wearing a grey tailored dress. Immediately
news of her presence spread over the house. The girls at
the top of the stairs called to the girls below:

'What is she wearing?'

They answered:

'*Une petite robe en Prince de Galles!*'

That is what the French call a particular kind of checked suiting which the Prince of Wales made fashionable, and I smiled at this apt nomenclature because the fleet-footed customer was the Duchess of Windsor! She smiled at the girls and hurried off to try on some shoes and the hat of red and black feathers that had aroused so much envy.

A young woman seated at a flounced kidney-shaped table at the top of the stairs continued to book appointments for fittings and to deal with requests for seats for the afternoon show. Content to spend an hour surrounded by beautiful things, I felt no more envy than I would have done in the National Gallery or contemplating the Venus de Milo at the Louvre. These people are real and vital—a lovely model, a famous customer, a seamstress whose large, wondering eyes make the fact that she is a hunchback all the more pathetic. When this poor dwarf stepped laughingly out of the lift somebody exclaimed: 'She is the gayest girl in the sewing-room. The doctors gave up hope that she would ever walk again, but now she walks. Is that not something to be happy about?'

An elderly American woman arrived with her daughter, who looked nearly as old as herself, but who, because she was accompanied by her mother, looked round each time she tried on a hat, seeking maternal approbation, with all the airs and graces of a little girl.

'No, darling,' said the mother, 'that one really does not suit you!'

Soon all the hats in the collection had been tried and discarded.

There was a bus strike in Paris. The inspectors and ticket-office clerks on the subway had come out in sympathy, but as the trains continued to run the subway system had become a free-for-all scramble. No tickets were issued or demanded.

I had promised to meet a friend who was having her hair done in the Rue Daunou, but on leaving the subway at the Opéra I suddenly realized that I was hungry and decided to lunch first. Opposite the Chatham was a small restaurant called the Rallye with a single row of open-air tables set out on the narrow pavement. The restaurant was very busy, but the table at one end was occupied by a solitary woman. I inquired if I might take the seat in front of her.

'But of course,' she answered.

She was a fine-looking woman with rather sharp features, a slightly too prominent nose, and dark hair that though dyed did not lack beauty. Her dress, expertly cut, had short sleeves and a *décolleté* which revealed the soft white skin of her throat and neck. Her voice, for she was quick to respond to my friendly overtures, was heavy with the Burgundy accent, and this evocation of rich earth was sufficient to tug at my heart-strings and make her a kindred spirit. I realized once again that these Parisians had deep roots that burrowed into the soil of their native provinces.

She offered me the menu which the waitress had just handed her, and I supposed she must be known here, for in response to a suggestion from the waitress she answered: 'No, I had some of that yesterday and I love to change.' She smiled at me and explained: 'I like something different every day. I shall have lamb with flageolet beans.' Her eyes shone in anticipation. 'That is a dish I can recommend to you, madame, for I can see that you are not a regular customer. The owners are amazing people, and what is unusual about them is that they took this place without any previous experience—and have made a success of it.'

A very pretty girl in a sheath dress hurried along the

L

pavement, brushing lightly against our table. Her dress was white worsted with grey stripes, the darts on bodice and skirt imprisoning her like a bird in a cage.

'What a beautiful dress!' I exclaimed.

'What a lovely girl!' answered my companion. 'But I grant you that her dress is pretty. Are we not in the heart of the "ready-made" district, with the alluring windows of the Samaritaine de Luxe at the corner of the boulevard?'

'I suspect that you are in the dress business?' I hazarded.

'Yes,' she answered, 'and indeed I sometimes wonder if I have ever been in anything else. I have been desperately interested in dresses all my life, and I am not tired of them yet. Fashion keeps one young. To be in my business is eternally to look forward to what next season holds in store. When the time comes for the great *couture* houses to show their collections, I work myself up into a frenzy of excitement. Their innovations make me cry out in admiration. Later, of course, I come down to earth. Cold reason must guide those of us who are responsible for launching ready-mades.'

'Have you a shop in this part of Paris?'

'No,' she answered, 'but I have a magnificent one in an important Burgundian town where I sell dresses, coats, blouses, gloves, and hand-bags. Window-dressing is a passion with me. I have a real gift for making a pretty shop window—and over my shop, which is in a fine modern building, I own the loveliest apartment.

'My apartment has everything a woman could desire—plenty of sunshine, a wide terrace from which I can look across the town to the country beyond, where the Rhône twists and turns between green hills. My furniture is beautiful, my wardrobes are full of dresses and hats, my kitchen is equipped with modern wonders, my apartment is warm in winter, cool in summer. Yes, I have everything, everything except . . .'

'Except?'

'. . . except happiness,' she murmured, lowering her
eyes.

She had looked so happy when first describing to me the
importance and prettiness of her shop. Then suddenly
with these last words the muscles of her face had sagged
and she looked miserable.

'There are moments when I would exchange my luxurious apartment in Burgundy for an attic in Paris,' she
continued, looking up at me. 'When one is alone—lonely
—there is companionship in a great city. The passers-by
in the street are one's friends, and even in a restaurant one
finds warmth and sympathy.' She gave me a quick, gay
smile of understanding. 'In a small provincial town things
are quite different. One cannot very well lunch at a
restaurant when one has the sort of apartment I have, with
a fine kitchen and all that is necessary to cook a meal. I
should feel ashamed. I should have scruples. Then
again it might not be wise from a business point of view or
in keeping with my dignity as a single woman. But none
of these things matter in Paris! Who knows me? A few
hundred business acquaintances! What is that in so large
a city? So there you are. I am tempted to sell everything
that I own in Burgundy and settle in Paris. I cross-
examine myself. I waver. One day I am quite resolved
to do so, and the next I hesitate.

'I realize that I have nothing left—nobody to love me, I
mean, for as regards money I am rich, rich enough for all
my present needs. Life by most standards has been good
to me. While still a girl I married a boy with whom I was
much in love, but I discovered that he was a gambler, and
though at first I tried to be patient there came a time after
the birth of our daughter when I knew that I could no
longer rely on him. He was, however, extremely intelligent, and had he owned the necessary capital he might have

become one of those financiers whom the world admires, and his love of gambling, which struck me merely as a vice, might have been taken for courage. We obtained a divorce. Left alone with my little girl I put my entire strength into my business, becoming, though I did not realize it at the time, as big a gambler as my husband, with this difference, however, that I was gambling with my own efforts, my own work. Fortune favoured me fabulously. Soon ambition crept in, not for myself but for my daughter, whom I wanted, year by year as she grew up, to be so much prettier, cleverer, more distinguished in every way than I that when it really happened, when she surpassed me in everything, she could not help feeling, poor darling, that I was beneath her!

'Yes—if I may be allowed to use an expression in my own trade—she is of a much finer weave! What is so idiotic is the length of time it took me to discover this. I was too busy. My shop took up so much of my time. Besides, one leaves the education of one's children almost entirely to others. After all it was what I wanted and it was entirely my own doing. However, it was not until she married a young man of her own high education that I fully realized what I had done.

'I bought them a magnificent apartment in Paris. Yes, madame, I bought it for them, as is the fashion here, and from time to time I call on them. They receive me very politely as befits well-brought-up young people, but I never experience that nice warm feeling that one hopes for when visiting one's children. I was probably wrong to expect it. After all, has one the right to think of one's children as being here for one's comfort and enjoyment? That, at least, is what I say to console myself.'

Her eyes filled with tears as, striving for self-control, she broke off a piece of French bread with the strong, capable hands of a successful career woman.

Ah, here was the pretty girl in the sheath dress coming back along the pavement. The cunningly placed darts on the tight-fitting corsage moulded her well-rounded breasts, and I loved the way the dress was buttoned. My neighbour, drying her tears, said to me:

'She is one of our ladies of easy virtue. There are several about here and nowadays they start work very early. I find it curious to reflect that while we women gossip over lunch, a great many men are already thinking about something else. Yes, even while the sun is shining! Curious how I used to think of love in terms of dark evenings and artificial light!'

She broke into laughter and continued:

'I had, after my divorce, a great love—and it was not so very long ago. One of those wonderful romances that bring warmth to the autumn of a woman's life, when one has almost given up thought of love and when one is more or less resigned to the idea of a comfortable and uneventful existence.

'We were both of the same age.

'He was an antique dealer, a very erudite person, and one is obliged to admit that selling antiques is a much more intellectual calling than selling hats and dresses.

'Well, would you believe it, he used to claim that I was as intelligent as he! What a welcome change for me, not to feel obliged all the time to ask myself if I was intellectually and socially matching up to the person I loved! Oh, how I hated those wretched comparisons! What intense suffering they can inflict! I began to enjoy in his company a period of absolute joy during which I rescued my poor heart from its feeling of being unwanted. My friend made even more money than I did, but in our minds the money we both earned was chiefly a symbol to show that we really were clever enough to make it.

'He had his shop in Paris, I had mine in Burgundy, but

we were always together, he with me or I with him. The mere fact that we were financially independent brought us nearer together, and as soon as we knew that we were irretrievably in love we were married.

'These autumnal romances begin softly but often end by being as violent as first love. That is what happened to us.

'When, after our marriage, we went to call on my daughter I no longer felt at a disadvantage, for was I not accompanied by a man who knew all about history, period furniture, and beautiful things? My daughter also began to look on me in a different light. I knew very well that secretly she was saying to herself: "Well, well! See that mother of mine! She is cleverer than I thought to have made a fresh start with such an intelligent man!"

'All this may seem idiotic to you, but it gave me an enormous pleasure. I felt warm and contented like an actress standing in front of the curtain listening to the applause of the audience. No, I felt happier than an actress. The approval of one's loved ones means so much more. I had suffered a great deal in the past—more than I was willing to admit.

'One summer after we had both worked hard, we decided to take the car and go off for a holiday.

'Business had been excellent, and neither of us had any trouble in finding suitable people to look after our affairs. If a business is well run you can safely leave it in the hands of your associates. After we had drawn up our holiday plans in Paris I left my husband alone for a few days while I returned to Burgundy to put my own apartment in order.

'Even so we kept in close touch with each other, and every day I would telephone to him or he would telephone to me.

'"I do wish you were back again," he said to me one

evening. "I have not had a good night's sleep since you left me. I am probably overworked. Perhaps when I am alone I eat too quickly or the wrong things. I think about nothing else but our holiday, and incidentally I shall take advantage of it to put myself on a diet. Fresh air, lots of sunshine, and you to look after me!" he exclaimed, laughing. "What do you say to that for a regime?"

'I was just as eager as he was to get away, but I thought he was making too much of his ailments. I told him not to fuss. "You will feel better the moment we leave Paris," I said. "Give me two or three days more to collect the right clothes, and I shall join you."

'I wished him good night and went over to my wardrobe. What dresses should I need for the journey? A woman of my age should not take her charm for granted. She should change her dresses frequently, for though it is generally believed that men do not notice what we wear, that is only half true. While incapable of analysis they remain extremely sensitive to the general effect. This was particularly true of my husband. I had two kinds of dress—in daring vivid colours, and little modest black dresses creating a more intimate picture, the sort of dresses that whisper in his ear: "I am a woman who knows that she is loved!" These I wore with antique gold and pearl jewels which my first husband had bought for me in the course of his wanderings.

'The next day I put a call through to him immediately after breakfast to ask how he had slept. "Worse than last night," he answered. "I was probably worried. I had decisions to take, accounts to go through, the auditors— I wondered if I should have bought those things at the Hôtel Drouot. I had eaten scarcely anything all day so it could not have been indigestion. Despite this, however, I had a curious pain, as if something was compressing me. Still, I am not worrying. We shall soon be leaving."

'I had so much to do at the store that I did not return to my apartment till late that evening.

'I do not know why, but I sat down and sobbed. I was horribly afraid. Afraid of what? I have no idea, but I suddenly began to pass under review all the many people I had known who were dead and what their symptoms had been. What frightened me most was a feeling of solitude. My wardrobe was wide open, but instead of continuing to fill my suit-cases with dresses as I had begun to do, I put them all back on their hangers. I went into the kitchen. Everything was so clean and tidy that I might have been in a hospital ward. I made myself a cup of coffee, but what I had hoped would prove a long, hot drink lasted only a moment, a mere trickle of warmth and life, and the table at which I sat seemed long and frigid. I could see my reflection in the porcelain tiles and chromium-plated fittings. There seemed to be something prophetic about my worried features and black dress.

'I tried to tell myself that what I needed was a hot bath, the joy of slipping into bed after a tiring day, and a nice long read before putting out the light. The telephone rang. A friend in Paris began to tell me in a strangely involved way that my husband had decided to consult a doctor, and that the latter had rushed him to hospital. "I think you would be wise to come immediately," said the voice.

'I flew to the station and caught the night train, but when I reached my husband's bedside the first thing I saw was—an iron lung. Two days later it was all over. He was only forty-eight.'

She cried gently, bravely, while passers-by hurried along the pavement. Her sorrow was already tinged with resignation. Her tears were those that one sheds after several years have elapsed since the loss of a loved one. At the time one's first wish is to die oneself, but alas! there is no alternative but to tread the path of life alone. Gradually one finds relief in talking about the past.   Memories are revived on the sunny pavement of a busy city street.

'When I talk about him,' she stressed, 'I feel better.'

She confessed that she worked harder than she had thought possible to assuage her sorrow.   There was something else that gave her new courage.   She blurted it out.

'I had my face lifted!' she exclaimed all in one breath. 'A tremendous success!   Did you notice?'

Her whole expression had changed, and she added:

'When I am in Paris and I have nothing to do in the evening, I board a coach at the Place de l'Opéra and go to the casino at Enghien.   I have dinner there and indulge in a little gamble.   I come back by coach just before midnight, and there is never anybody to blame me because nobody is ever waiting up for me at home.   I prefer Enghien to the theatre or the cinema because I like doing things.   A little flutter at *chemin de fer* is doing something.   I do not risk enough money to do me any harm.   Is it not curious that I, who used to be impatient with my first husband because he was a gambler, should end by doing the same thing?'

She laughed happily:

'I am going to Enghien this evening.   The night will be warm and beautiful.   Why don't you come with me?'

The apple flan at this restaurant was delicious.   I could see the owner's wife coming towards us.   Earlier in the meal my companion had invited her to join her over coffee. I finished my apple flan and called for the bill.   I had not the slightest desire to go to Enghien.   I had never felt rich enough to gamble.

I hurried off to the Chatham, where my young friend, Yolande, emerged from under the drier with what she described as a sensational new hair style, an end-of-the-summer-holidays hair style calculated to welcome the first

days of autumn! I accompanied her as far as the Concorde, where she dived into the subway while I made for Patou in the Rue St Florentin. A young woman who used to work for Schiaparelli facilitated my entry into this citadel, which was already crowded for the afternoon show.

Marc Bohan had created this remarkable collection.

His chief interests, he told me, were furs and little black dresses.

'Do not be taken in by the apparent simplicity of the little black dress,' he said. 'At first sight it looks almost pathetic, like an orphan child shivering at a street corner on a winter's night. One feels sorry for it. I will draw you what I mean on this sheet of paper. This crossover bodice is pretty and young. How do you like it? But wait! A little black dress is most exacting. As pork needs apple sauce, the little black dress needs a diamond brooch and a fur. The brooch lights it up and the fur gives it warmth.

'When I was a boy things were pretty tough in France, for we were living in fear of our lives under German occupation. I dreamed of the day when women would appear more feminine. Now that I am in a position to influence fashion I have splashed my winter collection with immense fur collars and muffs, for it is so often the useless, the unnecessary, that gives a woman pleasure.'

Was it just coincidence or the result of some current passing through the city that the two youngest *couturiers*— Marc Bohan and Givenchy—both wanted to make us more feminine?

This former private residence was quite superb, and the staircase was ambassadorial. The muffled roar of traffic sang in our ears. Patou's sister, with Marc Bohan as designer, carried on the fortunes of the famous house. On a table stood a bottle of Joy, that rare and exquisite perfume which perpetuated the name of Jean Patou, who in the twenties gave unforgettable evening champagne parties in this lovely house to display his dresses. As soon as the last guest had gone he would drive off to Deauville or Le Touquet to spend the rest of the night gambling at the casino. That was the decade of the Hispano-Suiza, knee-length, sack-like beaded dresses, necklaces that fell

below the waist, and a Montmartre of a thousand night-
clubs raucous with the feverish Charleston. Coats had
wide fur collars which nestled against our cropped necks.
Was the fox collar coming back? I hoped so! Dress designers are fortunate in that they can lead fashion merely
by turning the clock back.

24

THE fruiterers of the Rue St Honoré displayed large baskets of black Spanish figs. The street lamps were already lit and as I was alone I pondered what to do. Should I buy some figs and eat them on the balcony of my apartment at the Meurice? Should I go to see Véra Korène in Racine's *Athalie* at the Comédie-Française? I decided instead to enjoy the night air, seeking adventure.

Here was the Rue d'Alger. This evocation of the fairest of the French North African cities reminded one uncomfortably of the headlines in the evening papers. I recalled my first sight of dazzling white houses, omnibuses modelled on those in Paris, magnificent harbour, and Cours d'Isly, in whose wealthy department stores dark-skinned mannequins showed white dresses calculated to keep one cool under the hottest sun.

Now here in the Rue St Honoré was a small shop with a display of girdles and brassières of such exquisite workmanship that I felt ashamed to suspect occasionally that things were not what they were in a more leisurely age. Several of these pieces were worthy of a place in a museum so that future generations might marvel at our cunning. Some, made by hand, were worth small fortunes. The needs of the elegant woman are indeed many, for they include the invisible as well as the visible!

All along the street *concierges* were seated at their doorsteps as in my girlhood. Night was the time when they relaxed and exchanged news. No blaring radios or cries of children disturbed the gentle gossiping of these carpet-slippered men and women seated on kitchen chairs with their dogs and cats beside them.

Occasionally in a small café a few men could be seen playing Japanese billiards. I turned down a narrow street beside the church of St Roch. A shaft of rosy light came from a tiny restaurant which looked appetizing, cosy, and warm. Young couples dined at separate tables. There was a long bar with a coffee machine, liqueur and wine bottles, and a cash-register. Comfortable upholstered seats were built against the walls. The menu which was displayed outside was so tempting that I decided to go in, and immediately a young woman behind the bar called out a friendly welcome:

'Good evening, madame!'

A waitress, in a black dress with a white apron amusingly tied round her non-existent waist, hurried towards me. Her movements were so rapid that I had scarcely time to greet her before she had covered my table with a clean Basque cloth over which she placed a thin transparent plastic sheet. She informed me that the owner's speciality was scalloped veal with spinach and fried bread crusts. 'Excellent!' she murmured, turning her eyes eloquently in the direction of a young couple who were in the process of enjoying the dish in question at the table adjoining mine.

I felt delightfully warm and at ease. This friendly atmosphere was most restful. The owner appeared, exchanged a few words with his wife behind the bar, and then went back to the kitchen. The waitress opened a large refrigerator, which at first sight I took to be a cupboard, and brought out a slab of fresh butter which she placed in front of me.

Soon the veal arrived, piping hot, delicious. The young couple beside me suddenly decided to go to the pictures. 'The bill, mademoiselle. Quickly! Quickly!'

The owner's wife cried out to her husband, who was in the kitchen, that it was time for Micky to go for a walk.

'But I don't know where Micky is,' her husband answered.

'In bed, of course!' shouted his wife. 'Micky is no fool. He knows full well that these autumn nights are becoming fresh. You will certainly find him on our bed.'

'Very well,' said her husband. 'I will go.'

A few minutes later Micky arrived, stretched himself, arched his back, and jumped lightly on to the seat beside me. This beautiful Siamese displayed the intelligence common to his kind, and when I offered him a piece of veal he was polite enough, both towards me as a customer and towards his master's culinary achievement, to accept it gratefully and even, though he was clearly not hungry, to wait patiently for another piece. Then gracefully he leaped on to the bar, where he seated himself between his mistress and the coffee machine, undeterred by the hissing steam to which he was doubtless accustomed.

The restaurant began to empty and I told the waitress that I would take coffee at the bar in order to be near Micky. She brought me the bill, and a few minutes later returned wearing a poplin raincoat and a scarf over her hair, bidding us all good night because, there being no omnibus, she would have to catch a subway train from the Tuileries.

'And I don't want to walk too quickly,' she explained.

'Of course not,' agreed the owner's wife, 'but next week you will have a charming chauffeur to drive you home every evening.'

As soon as she was gone the owner's wife explained for my benefit.

'With her baby only two months off she is right not to hurry through the streets, but she refuses to give up working, and after all she has nothing heavier to carry here than a few dishes from the kitchen and the butter and the bread.   The kitchen is just behind us, the refrigerator is in the restaurant, and the wines and liqueurs are here on the bar.   So she runs no risk at all.   If she stayed at home knitting her baby's layette she would only fret.   These things interest me though they lack personal significance, if you understand what I mean, for Micky is the only child I have so far.'

She kissed him fondly between the ears.

An envelope with a Spanish stamp lay beside the coffee machine.   She took out the letter, saying:

'This charming young Spaniard writes to tell me that his employers, very rich people from Madrid, arrive in Paris next week.   They come here every autumn and stay at an expensive hotel, but their chauffeur lodges with us. That is why I told my little maid that she would have a young man to drive her home in the evenings.   He is most obliging.   And what progress he makes with his French! When he first came to us he hardly knew a word, and now he writes a fair letter.   I was amused because his employers had already written to engage his room.   Oh, madame, you should see their motor-car!   Our street, as you can see, is rather narrow, and whenever the chauffeur leaves the car in front of our restaurant nothing else can pass— the poor lad is worried to death that somebody with a push-cart or a barrow will scratch the paintwork.   Motor-cars have become so big that the older streets in Paris cannot accommodate them.   He finds it difficult to pass through some of our villages.

'Our young friend asks me in this letter to give him his usual room.   He dreads the cold, and the central heating functions better there than in most of the other rooms.   He also urges me not to reduce the price of his *pension*.   His employers are wealthy and can afford to be generous.   On Sundays, if his employers do not need him, he lunches

with us, and on rainy days he takes us all out to the pictures.
I might almost say that he is like a member of the family.

'In the evenings when he has driven his employers to the
opera or to the theatre, he comes back to spend the waiting
hours with us. We give him coffee and a liqueur, and he
tells us about all the wonderful things he has seen. My
husband and I, madame, hardly ever put our noses out
except to buy provisions at market, so we love listening to
his adventures.

'If he should happen to keep his employers waiting a few
minutes, the traffic being as it is, he can always tell them
that the police moved him on—or that he thought it wiser
not to stay outside the theatre because of the crowd. We
enjoy his company, and I am sure it must be less dull for
him to be with us than to be all alone in his big car!

'What always surprises us is how rich people, so generous
in some ways, cut their pennies in half in others. Every
morning, for instance, our young Spanish friend must call
at the baker's for two rolls and two *croissants* which he takes
in a paper bag to his employers for their breakfast at their
beautiful hotel. They are delighted at this saving. "The
rolls and the *croissants*," they tell him, "cost one-third of
the price when bought at the baker's," and besides, they
do not need to pay the 15 per cent hotel service charge on
them! So they just order their *café con leche*—that is
Spanish, I believe—and send out for the rest!

'We have a very faithful clientele, madame—only a few
rooms but always occupied. The expensive hotels can no
longer afford to have attics for couriers and chauffeurs as
they used to. The servants' quarters have been redecorated
and made available for ordinary guests. So the chauffeurs
come to friendly, family places like ours.'

An ice-cream woman was sipping a coffee at the end of
the bar. She looked in our direction and said:

'This cold spell has killed my business. Its suddenness

M

is what did the harm.   Unless warm weather comes back I shall be left with my stock, but it must come quickly, preferably to-morrow.'

The owner came in from the kitchen and said:

'I should be surprised if the warm weather came back to-morrow.   You have only to look at Micky.   Anybody can see that Micky knows that the cold weather has set in. He has not been out all day, the naughty darling!'

'If this weather continues,' said his wife, 'you will have to start the central heating.'   Then turning to me: 'Central heating is our chief luxury, madame.   That is why we have such a faithful clientele.'

'Yes,' agreed her husband.   'I rise at four every morning to light the furnace.   Then I go straight back to bed to enjoy some more sleep, knowing that at whatever time our guests get up they can shave in comfort with hot water in a warm room.   Chauffeurs who drive expensive cars like to be pampered.   My wife and I get up at seven to make coffee and serve breakfast in bed to our guests.   We have an understanding with them that any who have to leave early pay their bills the night before.   So you see we have nothing to worry about.'

'Well, well!' said his wife, emptying the till and stuffing the contents into her hand-bag.   'It is nearly bed-time, but the older I grow the less sleepy I feel at night.'

'I am the opposite,' said her husband, yawning.   'And just think how Micky loves to go to bed early!'

Whereupon the amiable couple and their cat escorted me to the door and wished me good night.

25

THE lift attendant of the Meurice—Castiglione side—and I were on excellent terms. This was because one day I had apologized for keeping my finger too long on the bell. 'I did not mean to sound impatient,' I explained as he was taking me up. 'I am not at all in a hurry.'

'Oh, but madame,' he answered, 'I am not vexed. Lift bells are very temperamental. I only heard you ring once.'

I discovered that he lived just outside Paris and had been at the Meurice for forty years. In his younger days he was in charge of the furniture, polishing tables and repairing them when they were damaged by guests or by a sudden change in temperature. Drawers, for instance, had to be tested to see that they opened and closed easily. Marble-topped furniture required watching. When it was nearly time for him to retire he fell ill, and on his recovery the admirable Mme Schwenter, who presided over the destinies of the Meurice, appointed him to the comparative quiet of this lift.

'She knew that I would not be happy away from the Meurice,' he said. 'So now I frequently have the pleasure of taking her up and down in my lift—though not always. In spite of her eighty years, I cannot be sure that she will not use the stairs!'

Then with the affectionate pride of an old servant:

'She is coming back to us from Switzerland this evening.'

The next morning I telephoned to Mme Schwenter in her beautiful apartment on the fifth floor, where I spent so

many charming evenings when her husband was alive.
She exclaimed:

'I heard from the lift attendant as soon as I came home
that you were here.   They have given you the apartment
immediately above mine, I believe—the one with the
balcony overlooking the Rue de Castiglione.   I am coming
straight up to welcome you!'

Two minutes later she was with me.

This very gracious lady had, in spite of my desire to go
down and pay my respects to her, insisted on coming up
to see me.

Mme Schwenter asked me, the next day being Sunday,
what I intended to do, and when I told her that I hoped
merely to rest, go to church, and perhaps in the afternoon
embark on one of those long walks through the streets of
Paris which delighted me, she said:

'Let us lunch together in my apartment, so that I can
tell you about the happy days when my husband was alive
and when the King of Spain used so frequently to stay
with us.'

Crossing the Place Vendôme, which was filled with
sunshine, the sight of Guerlain's in the Rue de Castiglione
reminded me that I needed some face cream.

A young and smartly dressed Spanish chauffeur was
supervising the packing up of a great quantity of boxes
which he would presumably take back to his elegant
employer, and I started wondering if by some amusing
coincidence he was the very same Spanish chauffeur I had
heard so much about from the owners of the little restaur-
ant-hotel near the church of St Roch. The salesgirls
made a great fuss of him, and when at last his parcel was
ready, tied up in the prettiest pink paper, he unfolded at
their invitation his own beautifully laundered handkerchief,

and held it out so that they could spray it with Heure Bleue
perfume.   Obviously this young man had no objection to
perfume, for his face showed the utmost satisfaction as the
girls stood round him, working their sprays like miniature
machine-guns.

In the Rue de la Paix I remained fascinated for a few
moments in front of the window of the famous shoemaker
Padova-Perugia.   One particular shoe had a delicate gilt
stalk for a heel.

For some strange reason I became aware of a woman
dressed in black standing beside me.   She turned her head
and we both emitted a cry of surprise, for she was the widow
who told me her life story when I shared her table at lunch
in the Rue Daunou.   I inquired if she had enjoyed herself
at Enghien.

'Oh yes, indeed!' she answered.   'An excellent dinner,
a lucky run at the casino, and an enchanting drive back to
Paris in the early hours.   What did you do?'

'I had a rather amusing time,' I answered, thinking o
the small hotel near the church of St Roch—the owner, thf
owner's wife, their Siamese cat, and the letter from the
chauffeur in Madrid.

Her eyes reverted to the shoes in the window.

'How extremely elegant!' she exclaimed.   'Did I not
tell you that in Paris one stumbled on something new
every day!'

She hurried off in the direction of the Opéra while I went
into the shoe shop, where a young woman accompanied by
her husband was trying on some shoes with very high heels.

'Those are very pretty!' said the husband admiringly.

But his young wife complained that what she really
wanted were flat-heeled shoes so that she could walk in
comfort through the streets of Paris.   She took off the
shoes with the high heels and tried on others with low ones.
Alas, her husband now lost all interest in her deliberations

and hid himself behind the pages of a financial journal.
His pretty wife was crestfallen. Should she suffer and
please him, or be comfortable and allow his mind to remain
wrapped up in stocks and shares?

She decided that love was capable of sacrifice.

Off went the low-heeled shoes. On went the others
again!

'Really, my darling,' exclaimed her husband, emerging
from behind his paper, 'you have the prettiest feet!'

He opened his wallet, and seeing that she still hesitated
continued:

'If they pinch a little we can always take a cab.'

She beamed. What did she care about suffering as long
as he was pleased!

I passed through the famous Market of St Honoré in
which were displayed fruit and vegetables from every
province in France, fish from the Channel ports, the
Atlantic, the Bay of Biscay, and the Mediterranean, and
meat and dairy produce from Normandy. Figs and grapes
were here in profusion, as well as the first winter salads such
as Batavia with their crisp white hearts.

As it was midday the dealers were thinking about lunch.
Their favourite restaurants, modest enough from the
outside, were in the small square. These gentlemen were
amongst the greatest gourmets in the land, and I decided to
lunch in their company at a tiny restaurant called Georges
et Bobonne, Georges being the husband, very corpulent,
who did the cooking, Bobonne, 'Merry-merry' or 'Goody-
goody,' being the wife. Small baskets in which cheeses,
of both goat and cow, were normally placed to dry had
been adapted as lamp brackets on the walls. A large
copper pan contained flaming gladioli.

A farmer-butcher, still wearing his picturesque apron,

joined a group of prosperous landowners whose businesses had obviously made their families wealthy for many generations. They addressed one another as 'thou' and 'thee,' and from their conversation I gathered that each owned several thousand acres in Sologne, Berry, or Touraine. Georges patted them on the back, was patted on the back in turn. They were friends, colleagues, all of a feather. As it was Saturday lunch would be generous, even more so than usual, and by late afternoon they would have closed their stalls or offices till Monday, and be on their way to their country estates to shoot pheasants, woodcock, or hares.

All about me these sportsmen recounted in their deep, jovial voices amazing stories of their valiant deeds. One of them claimed to have shot a rabbit at 250 yards. Another affirmed that St Hubert would not see him with a gun. Fishing was his sport. A third exclaimed:

'My week-ends with rod and gun are spoiled by my wife. A plague on these women. When I take her with me she ruins my sport. When I leave her at home she accuses me of neglect—and then it's nag, nag, nag.'

'You should never tell a wife that she gets in the way of a good day's sport!' said another. 'I have hit on a rather clever plan.'

There was an interested hush, and he continued:

'Just before pheasant shooting opens, I tell my wife to go to some expensive shop in Paris and buy herself a fine outfit—a stylish tweed suit, a hat, and a leather bag that later she will have no trouble in using for something quite different. Then I put a gun in her hand and take her along once, twice, even three times if that proves necessary. Gentlemen, she soon tires of that. She finds an excuse to stay at home. I plead with her. She complains that her shoes pinch or that her gun is heavy. So I go off alone to join the men—and my wife has nothing to grumble about!'

These gentlemen had their dogs with them. A golden retriever wearing a muzzle slipped away from his master to pay his respects to me. I passed a piece of sugar through the bars of his prison and he thanked me with a pathetic look in his large, humid eyes.

The little restaurant filled up. A young couple who obviously had nothing to do with the market were greeted by Georges, who showed them to a table near mine and then handed them two large menu cards. Smilingly he explained that whereas the card which the young man was looking at contained the price of every dish, these were deleted from the one he had handed to the young woman.

'Prices on a menu frighten the fair sex,' he explained gallantly. 'Women either order a dish merely because it is expensive, or else they go without everything they would like because they do not want to embarrass their escort.'

This corpulent *restaurateur* was extremely likeable. The rump steak with a marrow bone, the salad, and the goat's cheese which I ordered at his suggestion were excellent, and I had the strange impression of living in the days of Guy de Maupassant. Those big eaters talking about pheasant shooting, the stories they told about their wives, the golden retriever with the muzzle and the humid eyes, the owner's views on feminine psychology, all helped to create a warm, picturesque atmosphere, and I was delighted with my unexpected adventure.

What a lovely afternoon! The crisp autumn air smelt very sweet! I found myself reading the name plates attached to the big double doors of former private houses in the Rue St Honoré.

MME X, FORTUNE-TELLER—AT THE FAR END OF THE
COURTYARD

What a good idea! Why should I not consult Mme X?
The sun illuminated the paving stones of the courtyard
that must have witnessed the Revolution of 1789, and the
highly polished cherry-wood staircase at the far end was
equally old. I climbed to the first floor and rang the bell.

There were sounds of shuffling, slippered feet, chains
being rattled, bolts being drawn. The door was opened
cautiously and I found myself in front of a woman wearing
thick dark spectacles and a Chinese kimono of weird
design.

'Have you an appointment?' she asked.

'I was merely passing by.'

'Who gave you my name?'

'I saw it on the plate outside.'

After a moment's hesitation she said:

'Well, as you are here, and I am free, you may as well
come in. Saturday is not my busy day.'

I followed her into the apartment, where she went to the
window, removed her glasses, and looking questioningly
up into a corner of blue sky asked:

'Is it a fine afternoon?'

'Beautiful.'

'I seldom go out,' she said.

She must have been pretty in her youth, and her skin
was so golden that I wondered if she was an Arab. Her
eyes, as she turned to face me, struck me as having something curious about them, and I asked:

'What is the matter with your eyes?'

'Why should you think there is anything wrong with
them?'

'I am not sure why I think it, but you will have to take
great care of them!'

There was an awkward pause, and she asked suddenly:

'Do you want the *Grand Jeu* at 1,500 frs or the *Petit Jeu*
at 1,000 frs?'

What a waste of money! Secretly I was furious with myself. This piece of stupidity would cost me as much as a very pretty plastic purse which I had felt earlier in the day that I could not afford. All the same I could not go back. I would choose the *Petit Jeu.*

I took my place in front of her at a small round table on which she had carefully arranged a magnifying glass, a horse-shoe, a stuffed tortoise, and a pack of cards. I shuffled the cards and picked out a number of them which she laid out fanwise, trying the while to decipher my past.

She now asked me to place another card on those that I fancied. This I did, but I placed two new ones on the nine of hearts, and this appeared to vex her.

'Why do you do that?' she asked.

'Because the nine of hearts needs to be covered by two cards,' I answered. 'That, at least, is what I was taught.'

'How interesting!' she exclaimed. 'I should have guessed. So you and I have the same profession! Why did you not tell me that you were one of us? I wondered at first if you were a woman journalist. Your cards were so cluttered up with people.'

I refrained from making any comment, and she went on:

'You know as well as I do that most of our business is guess-work. One judges people by their appearance, the way they talk, the state of their hands, the jewellery they wear. One has to make up one's mind and then take a plunge. Is that right?'

'I suppose so.'

'The first visit is always difficult. Later on everything becomes relatively easy. One is able to influence one's clients, I would almost say to direct their lives. We even do quite a lot of good. Most people are incapable of taking decisions on their own. Between ourselves, I find it just as hard as they do.'

There was a ring at the door. She went to answer it,

and I heard a man's voice. She asked him to come back in
half an hour, and as soon as he had gone she hurried back
to me and said:

'You have brought me luck!'

At her request I chose some more cards, but again we
were disturbed, this time by the telephone. A long conversation with a woman friend ensued, in the course of
which the fortune-teller, as if forgetting my presence, ad-
mitted to great anxiety about her eye. The doctor, who
feared a cataract, had advised an immediate operation.

When she took her place at the table again she said with
false jollity:

'What a wonderful invention, the telephone! I who
so seldom go out can yet talk for hours with my friends.'

'So you are going to have an operation on your eye?'

'You guessed it the moment I went over to the window
and took off my glasses, didn't you? In short, you have
the gift of second sight. How truly wonderful! I envy
you! My gift is less sensational. I put people's pain to
sleep by a special form of massage. You might call me a
healer.'

For the first time I saw a small notice on her table which
said that she spoke English, German, Italian, and Spanish
in addition to French.

'The time has come for me to live in a warmer climate!'
she cried. 'I am thinking seriously of setting up business
in the south of France. Only one thing prevents me from
doing so, the thought of having to abandon my practice
here in Paris. The most important people come to
consult me, madame. If only I could find somebody
suitable to take my place.'

She looked at me intently.

'Somebody like you, madame!'

'No, no!' I exclaimed. 'That would not be possible.'

She put a plump white hand over mine, in an attempt to

convince me gently, pathetically, that on the eve of her operation I could not decently refuse to render her this great service, but I murmured excuses and fumbled in my bag for my purse.

'No,' she said firmly. 'I will not accept money from you, madame. Are we not professional colleagues, members of the same confraternity?'

I managed to slip a thousand-franc note on the table between the horse-shoe and the stuffed tortoise, and almost ran to the door. She followed me in her kimono, bidding me a tender farewell. Would I not reconsider her proposition?

On the polished stairs I met her next client. He looked a trifle anxious, almost ashamed to be seen going up to consult a fortune-teller!

26

I RETURNED to London with a new face cream and a tiny box of kohl which was my delight. Wise indeed were oriental women to make use of this black powder which gives brightness to the eyes, and must surely hold for us some romantic evocation of veiled women and harems?

During my last week in Paris I tripped and fell in the Rue de la Paix. My dark glasses, which hit the pavement, were not broken. I did not even ladder my stockings, but when the two men who gallantly helped me to my feet had gone away I discovered that my fall had quite shaken me.

A bruised knee, as black as a Spanish fig, which cost me several sleepless nights, gradually resumed its normal whiteness, but there was a spot, seemingly no larger than a needle's eye, that gave me a stab of pain when I touched it. I reflected that a week's rest in my London apartment would put this right, but day followed day and the spot was still there, as sensitive as ever.

I had not until then had any reason to take advantage of the health scheme to which I had been obliged for so long to contribute my share, and as I did not consider my case at all urgent, I consulted my local doctor and obtained from him a letter to the orthopaedic department of the Westminster Hospital.

London was beautiful even under grey leaden skies, and the bus which I boarded in the courtyard of Victoria station took me past the Army and Navy Stores and the Grey Coat Hospital, with the beautifully carved figures of a boy and girl dressed in the former costume of the school on either side of the royal arms of Queen Anne under the clock tower, and then along Horseferry Road to within sight of Lambeth Bridge.

The new Westminster Hospital, with its nursing and library wings, windows ablaze on this dark morning, stood out aggressively. I felt on beholding it an unexpected heart-beat of admiration. Here was modern science in the only aspect with which my feminine mind—hating war and its destructiveness—could be at one.

On the second floor, on the opposite side of the corridor to the wards, I waited in a short queue to hand in my letter of introduction to two girls behind a glass partition. There was a small waiting-room beyond this, where I sat in due course at the end of a bench beside a young woman who, sensing that I was new to these things, said gently:

'This is my final visit. I know all the ropes.'

She tapped the sides of a parcel reposing on her lap, and continued:

'This is a pair of orthopaedic shoes that would cost £12 if I had to pay for them. Of course in that case I wouldn't buy them, would I? The Chief—the surgeon who will be calling for us shortly—said I would find them a lot of help. When a woman is behind a counter all day she is bound to suffer from her feet.'

'Do you work in a shop?'

'At a big suburban store—at the hosiery counter; and if I need to be running about so much it's because—well, I just have to say it, I know the business better than the young girls. Judgment! That's what counts. I have it in the eyes. One look and I can tell what size stockings a woman wears. I never make a mistake. Funny thing is that a lot of women have no idea what size they take in stockings. Do *you* know, for instance? Shoes are different. We all know what size shoes we take but with nylon hose it's more difficult, and then there's the denier to know about, the thickness of the yarn. How many women know offhand that the lower the denier number the finer the stocking, or the higher the gauge the stronger it is? Many of my customers are important women, far cleverer than I can ever hope to be, but they know surprisingly little about hose. I am the person with experience to guide them. They will spend an hour choosing material or a hat but they like to buy their hose quickly.

'My department is very gay. I meet simply everybody who matters and in spite of a hot summer we were busy all the time. We work on commission, which allows me to earn a little more. That adds a zest to life.'

She paused while her eyes expertly appraised my own stockings.

'Very nice,' she decided, but there was a touch of hesitation in her voice and she continued:

'Did you buy them in England?'

'No, I was given them in Paris by Christian Dior.'

'Oh!' she exclaimed. 'I should have guessed, although that makes no difference to their size. I could have fitted you perfectly.'

She was called into the surgeon's presence, and, after inviting the rest of us on the bench to visit her in her store, disappeared. I edged up to a woman who for the previous quarter of an hour had been staring straight in front of her, and when I asked her if she was in pain, she answered in the sweetest Irish brogue that she was suffering from a stiff neck, because the men at her office kept the windows open all day so that she was in a constant draught.

'So here I am,' she said, 'unable, as you see, to so much as turn my poor neck round.'

I was about to commiserate with her when the nurse called out:

'Mrs Henrey, please!'

I was seized with a strange panic on entering the great man's presence. I had seen so many unfortunate people either on crutches or propelling themselves in wheel-chairs that I was quite ashamed of having so little to divulge, and even this little had been adding to my sense of guilt, because all the time I had been sitting on the bench, in spite of careful and tireless palpation, I could not once discover the painful spot, which seemed to have entirely disappeared.

The Chief was prodding my knee and I was on the point of tears. Nothing hurt. There was no spot.

To save myself from ridicule and to prove to him that I was not a liar, I suggested a final experiment. Kneeling in church the previous Sunday, I had suffered considerable pain and I hoped to bring it on again by the same method.

'Try kneeling on this wooden chair,' said the Chief.

I did so, and the pain immediately came back.

'Ah!' cried the Chief with satisfaction. 'Now I see what it is. You will have to be X-rayed.'

The almoner's clerk was a charming young girl whose hair was cut so short that she looked like the principal boy in a pantomime. She handed me a pink form and I was taken down to the basement, where once more I waited at the end of a pew.

A fat man, dressed in black, was anxiously questioning a young secretary, who clearly did not understand a word. Those of us who spoke more than one language did our best to help, but though we tried French, Spanish, Italian,

and German, he understood us no better than we understood him.   A waitress in an overall and a green cap, put
down her tray and exclaimed:

'Wait!   I will fetch somebody.'

A few moments later she came back with a short man in
a boiler suit whom she introduced as Bert.

The man in the black suit looked at the new arrival and
instinct told him that at last he was going to be understood.
He began once more to explain his predicament and Bert
answered him in his own language.

The two men, delighted with each other, went across to
a bench to examine a document which the fat man was
holding out.   Then I realized that the stranger was a Pole.
A word now and then brought back memories of the
black-out when Polish soldiers walked through bomb-
racked London streets.   When finally Bert had solved the
man's problems both of them rose, clicked their heels
together, and bowed from the waist in salutation.   The
waitress who had gone down the corridor to deliver her
tray, was now back and when we told her what had happened, she answered, laughing:

'Bless you, it was easy.   Bert's my husband, and he's a
Pole himself!'

One after another the patients I had met earlier in the
orthopaedic department again preceded me.   At two
o'clock I was given a card which entitled me to see the
Chief again the following week.   The main hall was
crowded.   This was visiting day and relatives were
arriving with flowers.

I sat on the bench beside the Irish woman with the stiff
neck, and soon a nurse arrived to usher all those of us who
had appointments into the Chief's presence.   There were
men as well as women and children in the big room, but

N

screens were so quickly and cunningly placed round each
patient when the doctors were ready to make their examination that there was little difference between this and a
private consultation.

The Chief was busy questioning a man whose clothes
hung over a screen, and I was intrigued by what they were
saying:

The Chief: Have you been in this country long?

The man: No, just a few months.

The Chief: Are you going to stay here?

The man: Yes.

The Chief: Do you think you are going to like it?

The man: I like it already.

The Chief: Well, at all events there is nothing new in
what you have come to show me. You must have been
in this condition for fifteen years. You had better get
dressed again.

Suddenly there appeared over the top of the screens the
smiling face of a tall Negro!

The Chief came over to me and scrutinized my X-rays.

'There is nothing to be seen there,' he said. 'What you
have is a small clot of blood which we must remove. You
will have to have an operation. The almoner will tell you
what to do.'

This great surgeon whom at first I had judged so harshly
now went to another patient. It was with infinite tenderness that he placed his hand on the woman's arm.

'No better?' he asked. 'We must try something else.
How long is it since you had your baby? Only three
months? Well, we shall fight hard not to separate you.'

Something was changed in my life. I was no longer
completely mistress of my destiny, for at any moment I
might receive a summons to enter hospital.

My nervousness translated itself into a desire to buy cretonnes.

I started by putting flounces round a deal table whose top I covered with the same material, but as I wanted a smooth surface—though not glass which is cold and breakable—I looked round for an alternative, something in which I could stand my baby Singer and from which I could easily gather up pins and thread. I decided on that transparent plastic used for protecting dresses and costumes in cupboards, and I was so proud of my inventiveness that I quickly decorated a trolley in a different coloured cretonne, sky-blue instead of pink. Thus my fever mounted till I ended by completely altering the appearance of my bedroom. At that time I was allergic to materials that matched, and as my room was small I preferred to look upon ten designs than one.

Above my work-table was a French poster with the portrait of Queen Marie Antoinette by Mme Vigée-Lebrun. The queen, in an exquisite blue dress trimmed with lace, held a rose between her delicate fingers. Copies of this poster, advertising the Marie Antoinette exhibition at Versailles, were to be seen all over Paris the previous summer. Beside my sewing-machine, which was covered with a blanket but always ready for instant use, I had enough space to write. There were plants in the bedroom which I tended like babies—three little orange-trees, grown from pips when I was making orange marmalade, which one day I hope to take over to Normandy.

Nancy Spain asked me to appear with her on a B.B.C. afternoon television programme, and this announcement was no sooner printed in the *Radio Times* than I received a card from the Westminster Hospital saying that a bed had been reserved for me in the Wigram Ward. I telephoned

to the almoner, who told me that I might keep my television appointment on condition that I drove to hospital
immediately afterwards.

I was overjoyed at the almoner's helpfulness, for my
only previous experience of a television appearance had
been in Paris, where it is a very informal affair. I was asked
in Paris to wear normal make-up because French viewers
like to see people exactly as they are without any attempt
being made to glamourize them. For this reason also
interviewers do not tell you beforehand the questions they
intend to ask. You must learn to answer quickly and to
extemporize: in short, to be yourself.

The B.B.C. on the other hand believe in interminable
rehearsals, and as a result of this you must report at the
studios at least three hours before your programme is due
to start.

I was to be introduced in a programme called 'Getting
to Know You.' We sat down in a 'drawing-room' which
reminded me of a doll's house, there being a background
but no front or door. A small sofa, a table, and a diminutive arm-chair were what I first noticed. There was a
piece of furniture at the back upon which Nancy Spain
immediately placed a toy tiger whose eyes were green and
cold. This was her mascot. Without the presence of this
animal something unpleasant might happen to us: a cable
could snap, transmission could be broken by what engin-
eers call a technical hitch. The tiger would save us. We
had nothing to fear.

The signature tune of 'Getting to Know You' was a
charming air from *The King and I*. Nancy Spain rehearsed
those of us appearing in it, first putting us at ease by
singing this introductory melody in her rich voice, lifting
up her eyes in a droll way. The cameras, looking like
prehistoric monsters, were immense one moment, smaller
the next, as they rose or fell, lumbered to this side

or to that, for ever dragging their heavy cables behind them.

Other performers besides ourselves were making ready to play their parts: a woman arranging some flowers; a small man with a beard cleaning a porcelain figurine; a pianist; a traveller from distant lands. Meanwhile, hair-dressers and make-up women arrived on the scene.

A make-up girl took me in hand, lifted my eyelids, and skilfully set to work with a brush as fine as the Chinese use to write their characters with. She said, as if to excuse herself:

'You know, Mrs Henrey, this really is necessary for television.'

'I welcome anything to change my appearance!' I answered. 'I am tired of my own face, but leave my hair alone. It is so long that I am the only person who can deal with it.'

Nancy Spain had taken off her jeans, for which she is famous in Fleet Street, and had put on a red dress and shoes with red heels. Her thick hair had been powdered with gold, and altogether, in this guise, I found her charming.

We went back to rehearse once more, after which it was time for lunch.

The dining-room was large, and Mrs Dimbleby, our producer, assumed the role of hostess. We were offered cocktails, but soon the room was so full of cigarette smoke that I lost appetite and ended by lunching on black coffee.

Two chimpanzees were waiting for us in the studio. One of them was to play the violin, the other to beat on drums. Their bright, intelligent eyes were full of interest as they looked about them, chattering away. One offered me a small hairy hand with perfect garden-party manners; the other put his little arms round Mrs Dimbleby's neck.

We played with them for a few moments, but they suddenly tired of us and rushed in a surge of affection to their owners, jumping up into their arms, hiding their heads against strong, protective shoulders, and emitting tender cries such as I have seldom heard even in demonstrations of love by children.

They were put on a small table and dressed in woollen vests and red trousers. I dislike the sight of animals away from their native surroundings. Zoos fill me with repulsion, and yet these two chimpanzees were cuddled and spoiled. The more I studied them, the more persuaded I was that they were genuinely intelligent. One of them, for instance, had been watching a woman playing the piano. A moment later he turned his eyes and saw her, still playing, on the television screen. Quickly he looked back at the pianist. Here she was alive. There she was an image. His eyes turned from side to side while his brain deliberated.

The one who played the violin took up his bow. His companion began to beat on the drums, but his mind was so fascinated by the living pianist and her television image that he allowed his drumstick to beat not the drum but his companion's back. The music came to an end, and several electricians offered sweets to the chimpanzees, but they would not eat them, coaxing their trainers until they gave them apples.

The minute hand of the electric clock moved towards three.

Mrs Dimbleby announced the programme, after which I was handed a pencil. My signature was to appear across the screen as I wrote it. Here it was in giant letters: Madeleine Henrey. I went to sit beside Nancy Spain and the camera leaped towards us. I was terrified. I hardly recognized my own voice. I had been told to hide my hands but could find no satisfactory way of doing so. Rules, I reflected were idiotic. Up went my hands! I

could only hope the producer was not looking. I felt
better then, but I blushed at the nonsense I was talking.

As soon as the interview was over Nancy Spain seized
her tiger and ran off to her dressing-room to remove her
make-up and change into jeans. I had no need of a
dressing-room. I should keep both my make-up and my
skirt!

'And now,' cried Nancy Spain, 'as soon as you are ready
I will drive you to hospital!'

27

I GAVE the reception clerk my name and address, but when she asked for the telephone number of my London apartment I was so exhausted that I looked at her blankly and answered:

'I have forgotten.'

'Do not worry, Mrs Henrey,' she said. 'You will probably remember it later.'

She called a porter who took my bag and accompanied me to the second floor. Here we met Sister, who exclaimed:

'I shall have to ask you to wait a moment.'

'Am I early?'

'No, you are late, but it does not matter.'

She showed me into a small room where a nurse brought me a pot of tea and bread and butter on a tray. Sitting alone with my bag beside me, I rediscovered my appetite. Ten minutes later another young nurse escorted me to the ward. The patient whose neighbour I was to be wished me good afternoon. Then screens were put round me and my bed. I must undress. I had finished being my free self. I suddenly felt very little and recalled in amazing detail my first night in the convent. My feet were cold and I was afraid of being scolded. The bed seemed high and I had trouble in climbing into it.

Then the screens were removed and a nurse unpacked my bag and put my things in a deep box built under my bedside table. A Jamaican woman wearing an overall and a pink cap was sweeping the floor of the ward with long,

gentle movements. Her swarthy features were grave.
There was no flicker of a smile.

To excuse the strange yellow make-up on my face, I told
the patients nearest me what I had been doing. They
were intrigued and anxious for details, and so I told them
about Nancy Spain and the pianist and the chimpanzees.
I became so bold that I slipped out of bed and walked
round in my night-dress. The woman opposite me was
doing some clever tapestry, another was knitting. There
were about a dozen of us in this pretty ward whose large
windows were so contrived that there was not the suspicion of a draught.

A man arrived with magazines and evening papers on a
trolley. I went back to bed, and my right-hand neighbour,
who was young and talkative, told me that she worked in
the hospital. I found that by a curious coincidence she
was secretary to my own surgeon in the orthopaedic
department, and that she was just recovering from an
operation. She had cut a corn and poisoned her foot.

'Can you imagine!' she exclaimed. 'With all these
expert chiropodists at the Westminster! There was an
abscess, and as I did not react to penicillin the Chief, who
gave me a terrible scolding, had to operate. So as a result
of my own stupidity, I have been occupying a valuable bed
for a fortnight.'

On the other side of me lay a very old lady. She had
trouble in breathing and a nurse was always near her.
She was seventy-seven, Sister told me, and extremely ill.

'I fear that on her account,' added Sister, 'you may have
a disturbed night.'

Through the tall windows opposite me I could see across
the dark lawn the brilliantly lit rooms of the medical
school. In what must be the library were shelves with
thousands of books. Sometimes a nurse, moving silently
about our ward, would pull the light green cotton curtains

round some bed, thus making a little room for herself and her patient. I was increasingly impressed by the trouble taken to consider the feelings and modesty of each patient, and my thoughts went back once more to my convent days. Had I by mistake entered some cloistered order?

When my companions dropped something from their beds they called Shirley. This patient was almost well and on the point of leaving, but she had spent so many months of her life in hospitals that she knew nearly as much about hospital life as the nurses. Shirley had become a sort of sixth form girl. She had a list with all our names and came from bed to bed to ask us what we would like to drink that night—warm milk, chocolate, cocoa, milk— and when we had told her she wrote down our requirements in a slow, neat hand.

I kept on picking up a book I had brought with me, but so many things were happening in the ward that my attention was constantly distracted. The nurses were very pretty girls. The fashions women discuss so ardently —Dior's latest line, Balenciaga's newest idea, the Oriental Look, the pencil line—all these were now forgotten beside the undoubted beauty of the hospital nurse's narrow waist, the full bosom, the tiny collar, graceful short sleeves, and the adorable cap which sits so lightly and prettily on the hair.

Everything in the ward was on castors. My bed did a *pas de danse* at my least movement. My combined bedside table and cupboard was also on wheels.

I left my bed for a moment and went off on another exploration, this time into the wide corridor where I discovered a row of telephone booths, and a ward similar to our own, but for men.

On my return, though I had only been away for a few moments, my bed had been entirely remade. The things I had left on it had all been neatly put away.

'Sister likes things to be just so,' whispered the nurse who helped me back into bed.

A rustle of excitement passed through the ward. A nurse arrived pushing a food trolley, and now Sister, like a grand lady in a country house, began to serve her guests. This was a cold repast but I found it excellent, having had nothing but a piece of bread and butter all day. The old lady on my left ate nothing. I listened to her difficult breathing and experienced a vague fear, but most of the other women in the ward had put on their headphones to listen to a popular evening feature. Our trays were removed and the curtains round the beds danced again as nurses brought basins of warm water to those who could not get up to wash.

Sister looked critically round the ward. Everything was as tidy as could be. My neighbours removed their earphones and composed themselves in a waiting attitude. There was an air of suspense. What could be happening this time? The orthopaedic surgeon's secretary glanced at her watch and said to me: 'In another minute you will see our first visitors arrive.'

My heart beat with excitement, and a longing surged up within me as if I had been here for days. How ridiculous! Only that morning I had breakfasted as usual with my husband in our apartment off Piccadilly, read my letters, and by ten o'clock had been ready for Nancy Spain to take me to Lime Grove. I recalled our mad drive through the traffic, the arc-lights and cameras, my stage fright before the interview, our arrival at the hospital, and my sudden sobering down from artificiality to realism. What a day! We all started talking from bed to bed, but our words were without meaning, and our eyes remained fixed on the entrance to the ward.

Suddenly a young woman appeared. She was in outdoor clothes and grasped her hand-bag tightly as if she were not quite sure of herself; and if it was something of a shock to her to enter our ward, it was just as much a shock to us to see a young woman in a coat and hat instead of a uniformed Sister or a nurse or one of ourselves in a dressing-gown and slippers. The young woman was followed by another woman, and then by several men and a little boy who quickly sorted themselves out and filled the room with the drone of low-toned conversation. At the side of almost every bed there now sat a visitor. My eyes turned back anxiously to the entrance. Here came my visitor, my own visitor. My emotion was such that I was on the point of tears. What had come over me? I was being idiotic. In short rapid phrases, knowing that our minutes were numbered, my husband and I exchanged information on the events of the day. He admired the ward, I showed him the box under my bedside table, introduced him to the surgeon's secretary, and told him in a whisper about the old lady on my left, whose curtains had been partly drawn because she had no visitors and was so ill.

Silence enveloped us. We could find nothing more to say. On occasions such as this the full flavour is in the first few moments. The instant of reunion is heaven, but as soon as the gush of words and kisses is over one can no longer be happy, for the anguish of separation already lies like a shadow across the remaining minutes.

The half-hour had come to an end, and we embraced. My eyes were filled with tears as I watched him go. Mrs Jeffreys, who occupied the bed opposite mine, was also crying. Her husband, a little man with a gentle head and white hair, had just walked softly away, and they loved each other with that fierceness and poignancy which come from long lives spent together, sharing every joy, every tragedy.

The last visitor had left the ward and nurses were busy at every bedside, closing curtains, pushing them aside again.

A young resident doctor, who for the last few minutes had been deeply absorbed in writing something at a little desk, looked up. He had new patients to examine, and to-morrow was operation day. There would be no visitors. Sister had warned us.

Shirley passed silently between the beds collecting flowers and plants, which she placed for the night on a tall shelf in the corridor. After this she came with paper and pencil to ask each of us what we would like for breakfast.

'And you, Mrs Henrey?' she queried.

'A lightly boiled egg is what I should like best,' I declared.

'There are no eggs on the menu to-morrow,' answered Shirley, 'but if that is what you would like I will give you one of mine.'

I refused vigorously, but Shirley explained that she was being discharged in the morning, and that as she had two eggs left she would gladly make me a present of one of them.

'How will you have it, Mrs Henrey? Two minutes? Three minutes?'

'You are wise to have an egg in the morning,' said the orthopaedic surgeon's secretary, 'for you will have nothing else all day.'

The young doctor, accompanied by a nurse, approached my bedside. Shirley was dismissed and the curtains were drawn. A thorough examination began—heart, lungs, throat, pulse, blood pressure, teeth. At Lime Grove, with the television cameras facing me, it was my outward appearance that mattered. That evening in hospital it was what lay behind the façade, the invisible mechanism, the muscular reactions; and the young doctor, taking a tiny hammer from his coat pocket, tapped various tendons, and did so many other things that I longed to question him. Why did he do this and that? I refrained, however, convinced that I should not understand a word of his explanation.

As soon as he had gone a nurse, wearing a mask, wheeled up a trolley. She expertly shaved the skin of my knee and then, taking up pledgets of cotton wool soaked in ether with forceps, swabbed my leg which she then covered with sterilized towels, eventually encasing all this in a thick, white woollen stocking.

I was permitted to take a little exercise, and I went as far as the telephone booths in the corridor to ring up my husband, who was surprised to hear my voice. I asked him if there were any letters, and after we had wished each other good night I went back to the ward, where I discovered Mrs Jeffreys making a tapestry with brightly coloured wools on a piece of Hessian.

'Mrs Jones over there is always very busy doing useful things,' she confided in me, looking slyly in the direction of another patient, 'but I am delighted for once to do something relatively useless. That is what I call having a holiday. As soon as I knew that I would be coming to hospital I set about collecting stray pieces of coloured wool.'

'I have begun to knit a scarf in shocking pink,' I exclaimed. 'I will give you some of my wool.'

'Oh, Mrs Henrey, how kind of you!' she said. 'I shall make use of it immediately, so that when my tapestry is finished and I take it home and make a cushion of it I shall think of you.'

Our ward was full of light and nobody wanted to sleep. The trolley came along with hot drinks. The day nurses left us. The night nurses took over. They exchanged a few words with the young doctor, and then visited the patients.

'Hallo, Gran!' they said to the old lady, but she had not enough strength to answer them. 'Hallo, Gran!' they repeated, and these two words were spoken with such tenderness that one would have thought that these young nurses were addressing their own grandmother.

A nurse now came to my bedside.

'I know all about you, Mrs Henrey!' she said. 'I have read the book about your farm in Normandy. How is your mother? Well? Oh, I am so happy that you still have her with you.'

She turned and said to the orthopaedic surgeon's secretary:

'Good evening, Jean. I hear you were able to walk a little to-day for the first time since your operation. Congratulations!'

Once more our ward became a scene of great activity. Curtains slid back and forth on their metal rails. The night nurses gently questioned us before tucking us up for the night. My own nurse was so small of stature that as she peered over the side of my high bed her face was level with mine. Her large eyes were filled with merriment.

'Sister wants you to take a sleeping-pill,' she announced.

One by one the lights went out, and as soon as darkness reigned over our ward I could see from my bed the myriad lights of the medical school wing twinkling as brightly as if a great ball were being given there, at which, unbidden, we might only gaze from a distance in our night-dresses, daughters of the house too young to join our elders.

I tried to settle down into the rhythm of the night, a strange uncharted night through which I was perfectly certain I should never sleep.

The night seemed as smooth as velvet in the half dark. I began to distinguish the beds and forms of my companions. I kept turning my eyes in the direction of the brilliantly lit medical school, and I reflected that if I were a moth I should certainly hurl myself against the window-panes in a stupid attempt to enter the bright rooms. The

poetic quality of the night was enhanced rather than
destroyed by modern lighting.

I moved in my bed. Little Nurse hurried silently
towards me.

'Mrs Henrey, you must take another sleeping-pill.
Sister says it is essential for you to have a good night's rest
before your operation.'

Little Nurse's manner was so full of authority that I dared
not voice an objection.

This second sleeping-pill proved no more effective than
the first.

Granny talked aloud and moaned. Her breathing was
loud, and from time to time a curious hard note broke into
it, a noise that I had heard before, but long, long ago—
when I was a little girl and my father, Milou, lay dying in
our torrid flat in Clichy. Was it the same? Surely, surely,
it could not be the same?

Little Nurse and a colleague were now at Granny's bedside. They pulled the curtains, shaded the light above her
bed, and gently changed her sheets. I heard them say:

'Come, Granny, try to swallow this. It will make you
feel more comfy. There's a dear, a real dear.'

But Little Nurse whispered to her colleague:

'No, she can't swallow it. We shall have to give her an
injection.'

Hoot! Hoot! Hoo . . . t!

There went a lighter, doubtless hauling a long string of
barges on its way from Brentford to Gravesend. Why
yes, of course, this great building was virtually anchored
on the banks of the Thames.

Hoot! Hoot! Hoo . . . t!

The melancholy night call of the river tugs reminded me
of another granny, my husband's erudite white-haired
mother, wife of a Brentford clergyman, who passionately
loved this river traffic which glided past on the wide

Thames flowing on both sides of a willow eyot at the foot of her walled garden. At night-time all this wide expanse between her house and the trees of Kew Gardens, with the red brick of Kew Palace dimly visible, would glitter with a myriad coloured lights, while tugs, trailing their load of barges, whistled and shrieked as they started their long journeys down-stream to the sea. My mother-in-law spent half her nights, occasionally till dawn, reading learned books, many in Greek or Latin, which her domestic duties left her insufficient time to read by day; and she used to tell me when I was newly married that she had become familiar with and had learned to distinguish each river call and noise. Nights were dear to her, nocturnal sounds softer and more familiar. Nights were her allies. The river whispered its secrets to her while she read her books and kept guard over her sleeping family.

Little Nurse had come back.

'Mrs Henrey, you are still not asleep. I shall give you an injection.'

I felt the needle prick my flesh.

'Nurse, why is the woman next to me having so much trouble with her breathing?'

'She is old and very ill. Now do try to sleep, Mrs Henrey.'

One by one the lighted windows of the medical school were dimmed. A patient was snoring in the ward but that need cause her no worry, for I should never know which one it was.

Granny let out a sharp pathetic cry. Little Nurse, with the help of a colleague, had just given her an injection. Granny was like a little girl. She did not know what was happening to her and so she cried and talked.

Little Nurse said to her gently:

'Quiet, dearie!'

Tring-a-ling! Tring-a-ling!

o

An ambulance! Down there by the river, coming ever nearer. We heard it enter the flanks of our building. The nurses were still with Granny, but by and by another ambulance came to us, and yet a third, and I heard Little Nurse say to her companion:

'It looks as if they are going to have a busy night in casualty ward.'

Had these people been injured in night work, run over in the street? Were wives anxiously waiting for them at home? Or had they nobody to wait for them, like the little old woman beside me who fell in the road and broke something, but was so old and forgotten that there was nobody but the nurses to care.

The voice of the river traffic became more strident.

There was a song I used to sing in my girlhood:

> Tout le long de la Tamise
> Il faut aller tous les deux
> Goûter l'heure exquise
> Du printemps qui grise.

Then, by an association of ideas, this tune was replaced by 'Sous les Ponts de Paris,' sung between the wars and now back in favour with a younger generation. The bridges over the Seine, the river traffic on the Thames— my two rivers which have followed me from girlhood to the present day.

'Tout le long de la Tamise!' I used to sing it when my father was so ill. Now I was more than ever certain that those harsh notes which crept so insistently into the old woman's breathing were the same that brought tears from my mother's eyes when my father was dying. But when I asked her what it was she would say:

'He has coughed so much that his throat is sore.'

Oh, dear God, how dreadful are the sounds of a person in the agony of death. Poor Granny! She was going to die. I had not understood. Granny, who according to Sister was seventy-seven, was a comparatively young woman when I last heard that noise. My father would have been about her age if he were alive to-day. I seemed to see before me a great curve like a rainbow. But what I knew for certain was that I should never go to sleep.

28

MORNING! All the lights went on in the ward. The nurses, like fairies, put an end to the night, dispelling its fears and darkness, by flicking their fingers over a switch. The façade of the medical school was now the one to be asleep. There was not a light to be seen in the opposite wing.

'Good morning!' said Little Nurse cheerfully, pushing a thermometer into my mouth. Now that the night was over I would willingly have turned over and closed my eyes, for I had used up all my energy thinking of people and things during the long nocturnal hours; but as soon as my temperature had been taken I was brought a cup of tea, that early morning cup of tea in bed which for some mysterious reason only tastes good in England. Outside, though it was still impenetrably dark, one could hear the first omnibuses, but Big Ben, which I had heard strike all night, chiming so melodiously:

> Lord, through this hour
> Be Thou our guide,
> That by Thy power
> No foot shall slide,

escaped my vigilant ears, either because of the morning activity in the ward or because the direction of the wind had changed.

I was allowed to leave my bed for a few moments, and I

telephoned my husband to tell him about the events of my night. He was asleep and could not understand why I woke him so early.

Before going back to bed I passed my hand very gently over Granny's forehead. Her poor face was like wax, her cheeks were sunken, her breathing hardly perceptible. Sister had placed barricades round her so that her body, lighter than a girl's, should not roll on to the floor while she was asleep.

Breakfast—my boiled egg had Shirley's name written on it in pencil, and as I looked up I saw Shirley bringing back into the ward all the flowers and potted plants which last night she had carried out into the corridor. She was already dressed in a skirt and a mauve pullover in readiness for her departure.

The newspaper vendor arrived pushing his trolley full of papers and magazines, and a few moments later our letters were distributed. I gathered from what the others said that because of Granny we had all had a bad night— and for six of us this was to be operation day. Two men brought an electric polishing machine, which as soon as it was switched on caused our beds to shiver and dance as it made wide circles over the parquet floor. I drew aside Granny's curtains. She lay very still, and the pitying glances of the cleaners who were passing their machine round her bed seemed to say: 'She won't last long, poor dear!' Their familiarity with death had deprived it of much of its emotional significance for them, but the West Indian woman who was using a broom looked at nothing at all, and I began to wonder what went on behind her swarthy forehead. Did those brown features conceal a craving for the generous warmth of a Jamaican sun?

The receptionists from the orthopaedic department, two pretty girls, looked in to wish Jean good morning, and I busied myself with the new scarf that I was knitting, but

though I also had a book I was unable to read it, and started
the same chapter three times.

Sister dispensed luncheon as she had dispensed dinner
the previous night.   An appetizing odour filled the ward,
but food was not for six of us, and we returned to our
knitting or the radio.   Sea-gulls and pigeons flew past the
windows.   The sky was full of grey winter clouds.

'Take off your wedding-ring and take out all your hair-
pins!' said the nurse, who then started to slip my night-
dress over my head.   She dressed me in a long white
cotton overall which fastened behind, thick white stockings,
and a mysterious emerald-green bikini, explaining in a low
voice as she did so that the idea of the bikini was to safeguard my modesty during the operation.   I was bound to
admit that the idea was both ingenious and comforting.

I was given an injection in the arm, and by the time the
first Wednesday afternoon visitors arrived in the ward had
begun to feel sleepy, though I was vaguely aware of strange
voices, and I dimly saw Mrs Jones being wheeled away on
a trolley to the lift up to the theatre.   My body appeared to
be floating in a world full of grey clouds.   I seemed to be
rolling gently over and over.   I heard voices, now distant,
now near, and suddenly there was a blinding light.   My
throat was parched but my brain told me that fingers were
searching for a suitable vein into which a needle could be
plunged.   In apparent difficulty they sought first here and
then there.   A soft voice murmured in my ear: 'Sorry, my
dear!' but what could I do about it?   However, I tried to
answer politely that I feared I was giving them a great deal
of trouble.   But my lips were so dry that no sound issued
from them, or perhaps it was that my muscles no longer
obeyed the commands of my mind.   The needle stabbed
my arm.   How easy it would be to die when one was

already only half conscious. The mask dropped over my face.

'Breathe deeply, my dear!'

Consciousness slipped away.

'How are you feeling, Mrs Henrey?'

A slight pause, then:

'We are in the papers this evening!'

The voice seemed to come from a mile away, but soon I distinguished the features of a young nurse peering down at me.

What time could it be? All the lamps in the ward were on, so that once again I found myself on the threshold of night.

'How is Granny, Nurse?'

'She is well, my dear.'

'Is she still next to me?'

'No, she has gone to another ward. You will not see her again.'

Jean, the surgeon's secretary, leaned over from her bed and said to the nurse:

'Show Mrs Henrey the evening paper. There is a piece about her being with us in the Wigram Ward. And a photograph too. Isn't it amusing for us all?'

I felt sick and my head weighed a ton. My knee began to hurt, but I made a pretence of looking at the paper which the nurse held in front of me. She was asking if I still had my farm in Normandy and how my mother was. These inquiries, she explained, were made on behalf of her own mother who read my books; but at this point I fell asleep.

My sleep could not have been heavy, because other voices soon penetrated my consciousness. Jean's right-hand neighbour was talking about her home. She was worried

because her son was to be married in three weeks' time, and
it would be sad if she were unable to attend the wedding.

I began to realize that for most of these women the
enjoyable rest of hospital life quickly gave place to anxiety.
How would their families make do without them?

Strangely alive to the conversations about me, I heard
another woman say that she missed her own bed.

'I had no idea,' she said, 'that my bed was so comfy!'

She added quickly:

'I'm not saying that we are not very comfortable here,
but it is not home.'

Her words received approbation and inspired others to
remark that what really worried them was the thought that
daughters-in-law, mothers-in-law, and neighbours would
almost certainly be poking their noses into their affairs
while they were in hospital.

'I hoped for a lovely time doing nothing,' said a voice,
'but how can one have a light heart, not quite knowing
what is going on in the home?'

Tap, tap on the floor.

Jean was hopping from bed to bed on crutches to inquire
what we wanted for breakfast.

'And you, Mrs Henrey?   Shirley left you another egg.
Would you like it?'

The thought of food made me ill.   I smiled helplessly.
Nurses arrived to prepare us for the night.   I must remain
in my white overall and thick stockings, but in spite of
a hot-water bottle at my feet I was cold because the bed-
clothes were raised so that they should not weigh on my
knee.   Nurses came and went.   Curtains were moved.

'Good night, all!' cried the nurses.

Little Nurse, who had just arrived on duty, declared I
must have another injection to make me sleep.

'You will feel much better to-night,' she added gaily.

'Yes, Nurse. Where is Granny?'

'She is dead, my dear. Just as they were putting you to sleep for your operation, Granny passed away.'

Dear God! So Granny and I both set off on journeys at the same moment—but in opposite directions. She went to heaven. I returned to the business of living. So that was why I should not see her any more. That is what the day nurse had meant when she told me she had gone to another ward. I was glad I had stroked her forehead this morning, for the gesture somehow made her seem less utterly alone. Perhaps subconsciously she had wanted me. 'If just once in my life a single voice calls me, I shall not have lived for nothing,' wrote Mariaud.

The corner she had occupied was horribly still, for her bed was empty. Another patient would be there to-morrow, and we should all forget Granny. Mrs Jones, whom I remembered seeing on her way to the theatre, was moaning softly, and a nurse in a blue cape, looking like a picture out of an old-fashioned story-book, hurried towards her.

29

SAD indeed for most patients were these hospital awakenings at six in the morning.

For most of us this was the hour, after a disturbed night, when at last we felt sleepy, but for our young night nurses this was nearly the hour of liberation. If they had felt momentarily benumbed by the chilliness of dawn, they could now joyfully exercise their youthful limbs. Briskly they hurried from bed to bed. There was no more whispering. They talked in loud, clear, girlish voices. Gaily they laughed. Their cool hands sought out ours, and with radiant expressions they comforted us, thrust thermometers into our mouths, and counted our pulses.

After the first cup of tea conversation between beds became more general and someone was certain to make a joke. We laughed easily, for there were no social barriers. Our afflictions made us equal. The nurses washed us as if we were children. My operation clothes were removed, and to my delight I was allowed to have my own night-dress and bed jacket. This transformation was in itself enough to make me feel better. The sheets were changed. I felt relaxed and drowsy, but there was so much to see and I was fascinated by the coming and going of these young nurses in their pretty white caps.

Breakfast and the morning papers. The tabloids were the most popular, and in one of these we read in bold type that hospital nurses made bad wives! Why? Because, wrote this newspaper reporter, they were too clean, too prudish, too fussy. This put us all in a splendid humour and we showed the article to the nurses. What amused me

was to read a newspaper story about people with whom I
was just then in contact. Bad wives! I looked round the
ward at those fresh, pretty faces, those slight figures
pirouetting with feminine grace from bed to bed. How
could they possibly fail to make adorable wives?

When two of them came to attend to my leg, I asked them
if they thought a great deal about marriage.

'Of course we do!' they cried out in unison.

'Don't marry too quickly,' I answered, with a very
serious expression. 'Think what a pity it would be to give
up a profession that you have taken so much trouble to
learn. When you are thirty you can marry some rich man
whose life you have helped to save.'

They laughed merrily.

'We want to marry young!' they said. 'We want love!'

'Love without money? Love soon blows away unless
there is a little money in the bank,' I said, teasing them.

Clearly they did not agree, and as they tidied my bed I
had to listen to a spate of objections. Youth was what
mattered. Love was everything. The rest? Well, there
would be plenty of time to see.

Delighting in their youthful optimism, I capitulated.

'Oh yes, marry young!' I cried. 'What in the whole
world is better or more important than a nice young
husband, a home, and a baby?'

'There are other things,' Jean called out from the adjoining bed. 'An interesting job is lovely too. I adore
my work in hospital, seeing new people every day—
patients, students, doctors. I enjoy every moment of it.
No woman could be happier. I am in one of the world's
greatest teaching hospitals, free from all those tiresome
household and family worries.'

The other women in the ward were unwilling to agree
with her, for was not Mrs Jones, for example, thinking
anxiously about her little boy who, in her absence, must

go to school alone, and was not Mrs Jeffreys worried out of her life because her husband, who was no longer young, would cycle thirteen miles that evening to come and see her in hospital—and thirteen miles back to his empty home!

Mrs Jones lived in Balham. Her husband was a chauffeur-courier who, working for a travel agency, drove wealthy visitors on sightseeing tours on the Continent. Mr Jones, because of his work, lived in a small hotel in Paris, but Mrs Jones, for the sake of the two children's education, had to live in London. Fortunately Mr Jones was spending his holidays in Balham, and this had enabled his wife to come into hospital, where she would have to remain for nearly a month.

A nurse was making Granny's bed and we watched her as she slid some fracture-boards under it. Sister arrived to inspect the work and when she had gone we asked the nurse who was to occupy the bed.

'Another old lady,' she answered. 'This one is eighty-one.'

Jean's right-hand neighbour, whose face I had never seen but whose voice had become quite familiar, exclaimed:

'Another old lady! Let us be realists. Nobody wants old people. Nobody wanted to look after my old mother. My brother, who might have done something, who was in a position to do so, refused. When we grow old nobody wants us.'

'Yes,' said another voice, 'if you want to be certain not to be left alone when you are old you must have a little money.'

'That's right!' replied Jean's neighbour. 'If I could have found myself a rich husband life would have been easier and I could have done something for my old mum.'

There was an uncomfortable pause in the room. Suddenly the woman repeated obstinately:

'Nobody wants you when you are old! Nobody!'

Our very pleasant-faced Sister re-entered the ward accompanied by her staff to serve us lunch. With great firmness she asked the librarian, who was amongst us with his trolley full of books, to come back later.

'I want the patients to have their lunch hot,' she said.

The lunch was excellent, the rice pudding well prepared.

As soon as our trays had been cleared we saw the nurses going to those of our companions who were to be operated on that day. Soon the stretcher-bearer, wearing spectacles and a little white hat, arrived with his trolley, which as a joke he trundled between Jean's bed and mine. Pretending to discover his mistake, he winked at us, set off again down the ward, and a minute or so later returned with one of our companions prostrate upon it. We all said good-bye to her, wishing her well, and though she was only half conscious she thanked us bravely. A wave of pity passed through the ward. Two minutes went by. Then another patient was taken away.

I asked a nurse when my new neighbour, the old lady of eighty-one, was to arrive, and she told me that she was being brought straight down from the theatre. My bedside table was gradually filling up with plants and flowers. There were cyclamen and violets and now an enormous bunch of roses had arrived, which a nurse had arranged in a vase. Before bringing them to me she took them round the ward for my companions to admire and smell. The woman whose son was on the point of being married knew a great deal about hospital life, and when the roses were brought to her she said:

'Yellow and red roses! They make a splendid combination, Mrs Henrey, but white and red flowers bring bad luck to a ward. Once when I was in hospital Sister sent back all the white and red bouquets. Carnations also are unlucky.'

Her words reminded me of a similar superstition amongst theatre folk in Paris. One evening, over supper, a famous

actress of the Comédie-Française had strongly voiced her
disapproval of carnations, telling me that she would not
have them in her dressing-room.

My roses were discussed at some length, after which
the conversation turned to love.

'Why don't you write us a real love story, Mrs Henrey?'

The woman who knew all about hospitals made this
appeal in the hard voice of one who had found life a bitter
struggle but who, with a heart that had kept tender and
young, yearned for stories of romance.

She repeated:

'Mrs Henrey, please write us a lovely love story, oozing
with love!'

The new patient of eighty-one was brought in asleep, and
the curtains were drawn round her bed.   The other women
who had been operated on were also wheeled back into the
ward.

I took up my knitting. The loose scarf I had been
making in shocking pink was almost finished. I had only
three more rows to complete it. The whole ward was
enthusiastic about this vivid colour, and when the last
stitch was cast off the stretcher-bearer put it round his neck.
Somebody else also tried it on, and then Mrs Jones asked
for it to be brought over to her bed. The scarf danced
lightly from bed to bed, like a message of hope, a symbol
of all that was gay in the bustle of city streets, in shop
windows, in stores, a symbol of brightly changing traffic
lights, of women tripping across zebra crossings, of the
delight which pretty things to wear bring to women.

The nurses were giving an injection to the old lady, who
cried out in a tiny, doleful voice:

'Oh dear! Oh dear! Oh dear!'

The night, my last one, was over. The time was a few

minutes past six, and the old lady, I am glad to say, was so much better that she was asking a nurse to fetch her ear-rings and side-combs.

'I would not like to lose them,' she said in a gentle but commanding voice. 'Also, please take care how you do my hair, Nurse. If you pull too hard I may lose some. Where is my handkerchief? The one I had yesterday? There is no need to dirty another.'

By breakfast-time the day nurses had relieved the night staff and my new neighbour was propped up daintily, and with great dignity, against pillows, her short arms crossed in front of her as in a Flemish painting. A slim girl, light of foot, dressed in street clothes, hurried in to kiss her good morning. Tender words passed between them. Was this pretty young thing a favourite grand-daughter? A wealth of affection lit up her eyes!

What nonsense to claim that nobody wants us when we are old. The things people say are not true. Generalities are false. Each thing has its counterpart. Grannies are loved. They do not always die alone. The world is full of love, and even if love stories eternally repeat the same thing, what does that matter? The evening brings despair, the morning hope. Carnations also are lovely flowers which come from God. How then can they bring us misfortune?